A TEACHER'S
MANUAL

A TEACHER'S MANUAL

Education for Smarties

Phyllis Tanner

To order additional copies of this book, contact:
Xlibris Corporation
1-888-795-4274
www.Xlibris.com
Orders@Xlibris.com

A TEACHER'S MANUAL

Especially for

ROSIE AND BENJY

LONNI AND JULIE

A SALUTE TO THE GREAT ONES:

Miss Palm
Miss Kendrigan
Mr. Faulcart
Miss Colahan
Mrs. Hartnett
Ms. Abramson
Mr. Caldwell
Miss Cotton
Ms. Tillona
Mr. Zaits
Mr. Howards
Mr. Buddington

And more, whose names time has, perhaps, erased from memory

With gratitude to friends and relatives, students and colleagues who cheered me on.

******

M any students, parents, teachers themselves, and administrators think that the #1 qualification to be a teacher is love of young people. It is not.

My high school language teacher didn't love her classes- or any of her students, for that matter. She loved Latin. She was intelligent, stern, and organized. Her voice was high and rather soft, girl-like, which belied her joyless presence.

Miss Latin was never absent and held to the same procedures every day: review the homework, explain an item that the class found difficult, teach something new, drill, and then do some translations. Each day, she appeared in a floral, swishy, silk dress and her business-like demeanor. We were awed when she broke from the routine twice, just twice, that year. Once, after listening to our translations of Julius Caesar, she remarked that, as the paragraph was of his belief in reincarnation, she, too, had become a believer.

Wistfully, she gazed out of the window and enveloped us in her tale of a bird that had recently appeared on a branch on the tree outside her kitchen window. She confided that the bird had begun visiting the day a close friend died and every morning since. She was lost in her thoughts and bereft; she sighed and shrugged with a soft, "Oh, well."

We stared, transfixed, pondering her bird- friend coming each day to comfort her. We could barely control our snickers (remember, we were seventeen). Miss Latin had shared, ever so briefly, a personal, a human reference. And what did it turn out to be? The most taciturn, somber woman we'd ever encountered believed an old chum had been reincarnated as a bird. Oh, my!

During the holiday season, Miss Latin handed out the lyrics to "Santa Claus Is Coming to Town," which she had trans- lated into Latin. We chuckled as she led the singing; and we fairly howled as we sang out the last line, "Santa Claus ad oppidum venit." It was light and fun; and, therefore, so out of character for her.

She loved her subject, was knowledgeable, experienced, and disciplined. I learned the vocabulary and etymologies, the grammar, the stories and the history. She never got to know us; nor we, her. She rarely smiled and actually seemed not to like us; yet I learned my Latin, and I learned it well.

Mr. Latin was my junior high teacher. He was dramatic, warm, charming, although strict. His voice could become that of a booming horn for discipline at times (discipline in those days meant that someone was not paying attention, gazing off in the distance, perhaps) and often for effect. His procedures were similar to those of Miss Latin: drill, new topic, transla- tion. He delighted us one day, when, as the school bell stuck and blasted for many minutes, he shouted out Poe's The Bells with grand flourish. Dressing and acting like a professor, with his tweed jackets that had those suede patches at the elbows, he had a presence that demanded respect.

Two different personalities, two solid backgrounds. I learned to love Latin and was prepared because, regardless of one's

7

lack of warmth or flair, they both knew well their subject. Neither of these good teachers befriended their students; they taught us Latin.

He enjoyed us, or appeared to; she barely tolerated us. They knew nothing about our personal lives or our aspirations, and note that I have called both of them good teachers.

THE MAIN REQUIREMENTS FOR A TEACHER:
Intelligence
Passion for the subject
Passion for learning
Education/training in the subject and in related subjects
Proficiency in that subject
A desire and ability to communicate
Maturity
Common sense
Enthusiasm
Energy
A sense of discipline
Patience
WITHOUT ALL OF THE ABOVE, ONE SHOULD NOT TEACH.

Now add, in varying degrees, these that certainly help, but are not vital:
A sense of humor
Compassion
Knowledge of other subjects
The ability to work with others—to share, to listen, to learn
Computer skills
Knowledge of the current world and the interests of the young
Education in psychology and sociology
Imagination
Creativity
A fondness for young people

Think back to your school days. It's not who was a "good guy" or who never made you work hard. It's not who entertained you or in whose class you always could fool around. It's not who gave you the high grade you hadn't really earned or who was "really cute," or nice, or funny. It is not-or, at least, it shouldn't be.

Think back and recall a class in which you actually learned, day after day, week after week. Conjure up that teacher who always gave homework and counted it, and went over it, and used it often to help you learn some aspect of what you were studying in class. Recall a teacher who was prepared and enthusiastic, one who both demanded and inspired you to do your best, not your fastest or your easiest, your best.

Which teacher afforded you many opportunities to "strut your stuff" in papers, in tests, in projects and presentations? A year's worth of progress, of learning and improving is what a teacher and a school owe each and every student each and every year. Didn't learn? Did you study? Did you try? Did you do the homework? Did you pay attention? Did you behave properly? Did you ask a question? Answer some? Did you seek extra help if you needed it? These are the queries to make. If the teacher did the job, the student should show improved skills and additional knowledge. These are what build self- confidence.

In 8th grade, I had a teacher who was notorious. A large woman, Miss French didn't actually sit at her desk; she ruled it. It was her kingdom, from which she never rose. Cluttering the desktop was an array of her daily necessities: bulky jars of marmalade; sugar bowls with dainty, little spoons sticking out; boxes of cookies and crackers; and a variety of napkins, no doubt, to brush away the ever-present crumbs. It simply wouldn't do to have crumbles mar those piles of French books, which lay "among the ruins."

Each and every day, without change, our class filed in then sat in our seats, while she checked the attendance. We thereupon went to the front table, where we deposited our homework, which I'm fairly certain she used to keep a home fireplace going. We took paper on our trip back to our desks and then looked up at the board to find our next night's homework, which we proceeded to do to get it out of the way. Interspersed with our lesson, were notes we wrote one another, sending them up and down the aisles quietly, so as not to jostle Miss French. She made tea, ate her lunch, or dozed, completely ignoring us.

We had heard for years about her routine, which was legend. There were no tests, no papers, no oral translations, no quizzes, no projects. Everyone got an "A" or a "B"; everyone was happy- incredulous, but happy. Did I learn French? What do you think?

Contrast Miss French with my high school English teacher, who was a gem, the best. Miss High School English stood probably at 4'6"-if that. She never seemed to walk but to scurry, rushing to the board or to a student to explain, to elucidate. Picture the stereotypical teacher of that era, and you have my role model. Her gray, long hair was pulled back with pins and combs to lie flat near the ears and then to swirl to the back to form a bun. Dark, silk dresses, patterned with bright, little flowers were her uniform, along with those heavy cotton stockings that looked like bandages. She wore sensible shoes, of course, black leather with laces and thick, wide heels that boosted her petite frame by two inches. I thought of her as a little dynamo. Her hands and face were pale and wrinkled. Her voice was warm, with a touch of Marine Drill Sergeant.

We drilled in grammar; we drilled in vocabulary. We had homework every night, and we wrote a great deal, as well. She recited poems to inspire us and had that presence that fairly seemed to shout, "Work, study, practice, practice, practice." She would correct the errors in our papers in red pen and give a fair assessment of our grasp of grammar and the expression of our ideas, believing both to be important. We knew she had read all the work thoroughly and were impressed that assignments and tests were returned in no more than two or three days; many, the next day. "The Little Dynamo" worked hard and was very organized, moving smoothly from unit to unit, prepared with enrichment material and reinforcement exercises.

It was clear to her classes, regardless of the course or the designation, that she held all her students to a high standard. An "A" from her was a coveted prize, for it was earned through scholarship, which meant work and study. Not to do what she required was tantamount to sin.

We learned our vocabulary words and how to use them effectively in our papers. We became proficient with the grammar. We reveled in Shakespeare and delighted in poetry with her. Our essays began to take on some intelligence and some originality. Our confidence was buoyed because it was clear to each of us that we were improving—and enjoying the adventure of it. That was it: she made it, our progress and the class, an adventure, not by befriending us, surely not, but by setting out in front of us, as on a buffet table, the items that we needed to comprehend, to savor and to master. The regimentation, the repetition, with small doses of variety and inspiration, empowered us; and we knew it.

One day on her desk, at which she rarely sat during class, was a small vase with bunch of dark purple flowers. A girl asked what they were. Joyously, with a pixyish grin, she recited Emerson's "Rhodora," which we then discussed briefly. So impressive was she to burst into an apt poem, for we had been discussing beauty and nature. Just another bit of inspiration. To this day I can recite the poem; to this day I am moved by it.

I have used this poem that I "discovered" in her class in my poetry unit in my own classes. I feel a connection to her still and to my 9th grade English teacher, as well. These intelligent, firm yet warm, women reinforced my own desire to teach, to emulate them.

Do you know Edna St. Vincent Millay's sonnet about the young woman who yearns not to play the games of romance, nor to proffer the empty promises of relationships? She speaks of "Love in the open hand, no thing but that, ungemmed, unhidden, wishing not to hurt..."

These two gray-haired, middle-aged women, along with several others, stoked a passion in me with their passion, their sense of discipline, their high expectations, and their keen intellect. I felt brimming with so much to offer that I wanted to call out, just as the woman in the poem does, "Look, my classes, 'Look what I have! -And these are all for you.' "

Teachers have, as do we all, individual personalities, styles, and idiosyncrasies. I have observed rather dry, quiet, and structured teachers who taught well, meaning they helped their students learn; and never was there any doubt in their students' minds as to what they were there for. On the other hand, there are some fine teachers who are imbued with a dramatic presence, with the talent of a performer or an orator. I have watched teachers who are beguiling, rife with charm. The point is that learning has to depend on elements, such as structure, routine, drill, study, and organization because every teacher cannot be, is not a highly charged, demonstrative source of inspiration. Even those who are, are not thus every day.

There are teachers who, although they have intelligence and a sense of style, simply are not good teachers. Haven't you ever had teachers who were pleasant and certainly bright, but confused caring for rigor and concern for organization? They entertained and were memorable, but too many of their pupils did not learn. And why didn't they learn? They were not made to; they did not have to. But they all got high grades. "And he was such a swell guy."

There are also many who do have that zest, that panache, and weave it in, remembering that it is an aid, a tool to help students learn what they are there to learn. Much of teaching is theater.

You see, along with the sincerity or the drama or the camaraderie of some educators, there must be consistently (yes, you've got it) the discussion, the homework, the drill, the exams, the papers, the assigned study; for, without all of the latter, the former is dash or a flicker.

"GET THE LITTLE BOOK." William Strunk, Jr.

In the same fashion that writers and teachers use *Elements of Style*, I hope, with great humility, that *A Teacher's Manual* will become a guide to those aspiring to become teachers and those on the job.

Parents could utilize it, assessing classroom management of their children's classes and schools.

School Committees could read it and "get a feel" for the operations of the classroom and the challenges their faculties face. It could help them set goals and be an aid in judging the performance of teachers.

Colleges, preparing students for the field of education, could use it as a tool for discussion and as an aid in "student teaching" courses.

Politicians might better grasp the importance of the role of the teacher, as well as the many tasks the schools are asked to accomplish, the place for technology and for student testing, etc.

51-TANN

I am not sui generis—there are thousands of experienced, bright, creative, hard working, dedicated educators in our public schools. Let's ensure they all are.

There is, to my knowledge, no such teachers' guide to assist teachers. My colleagues say they are anxious to have a copy to help them do their jobs; they respected the job I did and, evidently, think I have some worthwhile advice to pass on to them.

A Teacher's Manual is that: my advice, my observations, my predictions, along with my fervent wish that our young people receive the best education, not an adequate education, not rhetoric. They deserve an education that is superlative, taught by gifted teachers.

For more than thirty years, I've heard about our desire to have the best facilities, the most up-to-date texts, state of the art technology, and the highest caliber of educators, who are well paid and well respected. *Enough! Let's do it—already!*

"To Strive, To Seek, To Find, And Not To Yield."

Alfred Lord Tennyson

"Our Schools Should Be Palaces."

Aaron Sorkin

Contents

ADDENDUM

PREFACE

Teaching is my passion and my joy. I delight in opening new worlds for others—and for me. To share my years as a teacher with those who teach or desire to teach, those interested in education, in young people—is a delight. I want to keep it simple and honest, hoping that you will find some helpful advice within these pages.

As I counsel my students, do not be dismayed that newspapers are not filled with "happier, more positive" stories. You will find those, as well; but the warnings, the lessons of life often come with dramas, the action, and the mistakes. They stir our imagination and peak our interest. They also spur examination and change.

Here I relay the "tales from the trenches," so to speak. Know that there are thousands of gifted teachers (and I taught with some of them), doing creative and wondrous lessons and, perhaps, more importantly, doing the daily, solid teaching, day after every day, which must take place if there is to be genuine learning. To aid you in benefiting from the successes and avoiding the pitfalls, I offer *A Teacher's Manual*.

Teachers are considered small change—make no mistake about it; all the rhetoric to the contrary is just that, rhetoric. We must make the career of teaching known as what it really is—art, craft, and a noble profession. We must entice the brightest, the most enthusiastic and most ambitious to become teachers. A climate of respect for educators, inside the schools and "out into our nation" must be built. It does not

---

21

exist now. Salaries must reflect that great teachers are creators, valued and admired.

Public education must improve for everybody, and fine teachers can help make that happen. This country cannot afford to have schools become facilities solely for the poor and undereducated, while the middle class and the rich enroll their children by the droves in private or parochial schools.

This is not what we want for our country. **We seek— again—the promise of excellence from our public schools. Our children deserve no less.**

I LOVE TEACHING—
THE MISSION

I sat in on an interview, as the school Principal was questioning an applicant. They laughed and joked and chatted. He is a very personable, rather charming man: she is pretty, young, eager. He conducted the interview, and I observed, as English Department Head. She had solid credentials, having recently been graduated from a good state university, and was currently working at a summer day camp as a counselor. He turned to me, now that some of his background questions were concluded, asking if I had anything to add. Well, certainly I had; for nothing had been asked about "English"; queries by him about her student teaching had elicited only, "I just loved it."

It went something like this:
Me: Who are your favorite writers?
Applicant: Well, I really don't have any. (She and the Principal both laugh.)
Me: You're applying for an English job; you must read someone, something. What about current authors?
Applicant: (Giggle) I really don't read much. I don't know any current authors.

Me: What about journalists? What newspapers do you read?
Magazines? Who are you favorite columnists?
(Big grin and a hair-toss, as now they both titter)
Applicant: It's August, and I've been out of school for about
four months. I'm just relaxing and having fun, and I just
haven't done any reading. (Big smile, not at me, but at
him, as they nod in agreement.

I felt secure in the fact that that this young woman was
not going to get the job. Alas, silly me.

An English major who doesn't read? Not the classics, not
current works, not newspapers, not magazines? What? Had
she determined that I was rather an inconsequential figure
and that the answers to my questions were immaterial? That
I was the fuddy-duddy Department Head; but he, affable he,
was the decision-maker? Did she not realize that people should
read? Was she so detached that she was unaware that an English teacher, especially, should read—and should want to?
Doubly sad to me was that she appeared oblivious to the fact
that, not only was she not a reader, a lover of the written
word, but that she was not alert enough to know that she
should be. At the very least, one would think she should be
clever enough to say that she was.

She, no doubt, would counter with the fact that she was
being honest. Some of my students occasionally felt that, even
though what they did was wrong, there should be no conse-
quences because they told the truth. "I didn't do my homework, but I shouldn't be marked down because I didn't lie
about it." Sure!

The next candidate was sweet, quietly attractive, and
experienced. She rattled off a list of her favorite writers. We
chatted about several of them, their works and their styles.
She wasn't as young, as pretty, or as perky. She also would
have commanded about two thousand more dollars, due to

her work history. Although more prepared, more experienced, and manifestly more mature, she was not hired.

The giggling, vivacious woman (who stated she was simply too busy to read) was hired and did, in fact, "love her kids." Their learning, their scholarship was not foremost on her agenda, however. Their happiness, their confidences about their loves and lives were her priority. She wanted to be popular with her charges, to be loved.

An English teacher's job is to help students improve their writing skills, their oral communication, to help them learn about literature, authors, styles, the history. The young people are there to become more proficient with the bounty of literature, the ideas, the vocabulary, and the grammar. If you work hard, creatively and efficiently, your students will show progress and, along the way, (we fervently hope) will develop a deeper understanding of and a greater appreciation for their language. They will, with some inspiration and opportunity, find their own voices. If a teacher hasn't tried to do all that, she hasn't done her job, the one for which she was hired.

Then we have the handsome, energetic rookie, a teacher of computers and a coach. Walking in one humid morning in June, I encounter Mr. Energy. We exchange greetings; and, making small talk, I comment on the bright, sunny day. He responds, flashing a great grin, "It certainly is a day that will live in infamy alright." It's a what? This caliber of intellect populates teaching in small numbers within the last decade or more—up to the present. No, it isn't all, by any means. It's too many, however.

Colleges lowered their standards; public schools at every grade level lowered their standards. We fought for inclusion of special needs students into almost every class. We added little-to-no new funding. We smiled and bragged, as we sought to wire every school, then every classroom onto the Net. It was as though those in charge believed that this modern wonder, which it is, could study and learn for our students. We didn't hire more teachers or many highly qualified teachers or administrators, and we didn't supervise the ones we had. We didn't praise them, nor pay them well, nor entice many bright lights to enter the profession. We didn't—and don't—realize that, as Joan Vennochi of the *Boston Globe* headlined, "More testing doesn't mean better education." We didn't tighten up on discipline; and then we are shocked—shocked, I tell you—that so many of our students fared so poorly on the state testing. Well!

This is the harvest we've reaped. Yet we are appalled at the results of statewide testing. How could it have been otherwise?

I LOVE TEACHING

I love teaching, always did; I felt I was born to teach. It often was my "natural high." Finding ways to help young people learn, exploring texts to share, methods to use –all were invigorating. There were times of frustration and helplessness, but I ended countless days with a feeling of warmth and accomplishment, knowing that much of the day was actual pleasure. It was taxing, yet fun. No, I didn't spin around like a whirling dervish; but I was so cognizant of the fact that this was a good day, a day that a student "turned around," a day that the discussion was animated, a day that they sounded like mini-experts on the unit's subject. And, yes, I often ambled, singing some tune, down the long corridors.

I want the reader to see through my eyes my realities, not the rhetoric nor the hype of politicians and administrators. Teaching for more than thirty years, I want to pass on some advice, some suggestions, and some observations. I hope that experienced teachers, new teachers, administrators, and parents can gain from my background. For a long time, I really didn't connect to the fact that this was my living, that this paid the mortgage, perhaps, because I enjoyed it so much.

Teaching has a mystique about it. Americans look with nostalgia, on the whole, to our own schooling, our youthful, spirited years in the classroom. We also are aware of the importance of education today and in the future. We are armed with CNN's "factoids" of the percent of workers needing

---

27

new skills; the future elimination of jobs that simply will no longer exist; the higher pay of those with diplomas, with training, degrees, advanced degrees, etc. We're disillusioned with our schools today, partly because we invest so much hope in them.

We ask our schools to be our panaceas; and, therefore, entrust them with the tasks of solving society's ills, of confronting so many problems:

Crime and violence
Disrespect for authority
Illegitimacy
Teen pregnancy
Drug abuse
Spousal abuse
Unsafe sex
Promiscuity
Smoking
Racism
Voter apathy
Alcohol abuse
Malnutrition
Class structure
Peer pressure
Sexism
Homophobia
Incivility
Drunk driving
AIDS
Low self-esteem
Prejudice
Anorexia/ Bulimia
Lack of values
Poor parenting skills
Sexual harassment

Believe it or not, there are courses, lessons, classes, and/ or programs in all the above.

Add to this litany, these academic challenges, along with a regular curriculum:

Understanding our country's history, traditions, and literary heritage, as well as world history, since the latter and the former are so linked, so entwined.

Proficiency in science and math

Mastery of communication skills: writing and speaking

Proficiency in technology

Mastery of reading skills

What a myriad of roles the schools are asked to play. Here is my child. Teach him to read and write, of course. Teach him mathematics and about the natural/scientific world around him. Teach him about our land and foreign lands, as well. Expose him to other languages. Let him learn how to behave and how to play and work with others. Bring to him the world of the arts: drama, music, and art, to allow him both to appreciate their beauty and to give him opportunities for his own expression. Engage him in exercise and opportunities for physical competition. Teach him the importance of health and nutrition. Alert him to the multitude of dangers that may face him in a complex world, so he is armed with information and behavioral choices to protect himself.

Remember you have him five days a week; so there is much you can show him of the joys of the world, the laughter and the fun. And don't forget we want him to grow up to be a good citizen and to develop commendable qualities, such as honesty and dependability. Foremost, perhaps, is our desire that he have facility with his own language, its lexicon, usage, and literary heritage.

In an increasingly technological world, the computer must

be mastered and utilized in many courses. This and more you are hereby mandated to do with intelligence and a kind nature. We also expect that he will "feel good about himself," while going about all this, which, too, is part of your job.

* * *

The job of the teacher is to do her job. Simplistic? Not really. A teacher has to teach that subject for which she was hired. Yes, you will relate ideas to the students' world; and, yes, you will make relevant the facts and ideas that you are teaching; but, above all, you will help students learn the skills of the course you were hired to teach.

In graduate school, a student, who was an English teacher, confided to the professor and to the class that she was called to make bail for one of her students and that she had tried, in and out of class, to help him with his problems. He was engaged in criminal activity and had very little family support, so she felt that it was her duty to step into the breach. She wanted advice on how to handle the situation and wanted praise, as well, for "being there" for her pupil.

The professor asked whether she had consulted the guidance counselor, the social worker, the principal, the school psychologist—anyone—in her school about the boy? She had not. He explained that a teacher did become, occasionally, a sounding board, a confidant, and an advisor; but, on the whole, he did not recommend getting into that mode consistently.

"There are people with expertise and experience, trained to help that boy, right there within your building, within your system," he insisted. "Your good intentions should have pointed the boy in the direction of these professionals," he continued. She was rather aghast; for she was proud of herself that, for many weeks, she had been his support system.

"But did you teach others in his class their English skills?

Or were you preoccupied? Did he progress during this time in English, which he probably needed desperately?" He went on, noting that some students do have such weighty problems that concentrating on the subjects becomes difficult, if not impossible. You are there to help students learn your subject, in the same manner that others in your school and in your system are present to aid youngsters in crisis and those with problems.

His point, drummed over and over, was true then and true today: do the job for which you were hired. That is your vocation; for a teacher, that is your mission.

I am aware that I keep repeating what should be obvious; therefore, understand, please, that it is not. There are too many distractions, too many scenarios of teachers neglecting (shall we call it "benign neglect?") their actual daily teaching duties in favor of being charming, sympathetic, well-liked, or "one of the guys."

THE 50+ TEACHING GUIDELINES

You will meet the most interesting, young people. Some will be amiable and warm; others will be shy and reticent. There will be those, who are just bursting with enthusiasm and vivacity, sitting right next to a bundle of apathy or downright hostility. Some will be bright and cooperative; others, not so bright and not so cooperative. They are growing and changing—a potpourri every day.

Think of yourself as fortunate. You, if this truly is the career for you, are entrusted to help hundreds, maybe thousands, of young people learn. Most of them will be a pleasure, making your workday fly by. A few will give you "a run for your money," almost daring you to try to teach them. The challenge is that you are to teach them all, give up on no one, and try to find the key, the magic to help each one learn that subject, stretch that mind, and ignite that ability. It's not only that "[their] reach should exceed [their] grasp"; their grasp must become more able, thus, more confident.

This will take all of your training and intelligence. It will help if you are patient and understanding. (How's that for an understatement?) But, make no mistake about it, those students need you to be knowledgeable and firm, aware of what is going on in your classroom. A teacher must focus on the fact that students are in class because what you have to teach them is important for them to know.

———

It is, I believe, a noble mission (yes, I previously stated this!). It often was—truly—euphoria; it always was hard work.

* * *

1. MAKE VOCABULARY AN INTEGRAL PART OF THE COURSE

The language and ideas we use to communicate with one another are important. Make it so not only by stating that, but also by giving credit to those who utilize their "new" words in their speaking, their writing, and their testing. An extra consideration should be afforded, and marked into the rank book, to those who bring in pertinent articles, which contain "their words" from daily newspapers or weekly magazines. Connecting class work to the "outside world" by recognizing the vocabulary words and/or the ideas discussed in class should receive notice—"loud and clear."

PNEUMONOULTRAMICROSCOPICSILICO VOLANOCONEOSIS, HEBETUDINOUS, AND ERUDITE—if you please

Words can be fun, so interesting and so useful. Words, powerful in themselves as tools for expression, also give the "owner" power and confidence. "Big" words delight young people, perhaps all people.

Knowing early on that students can take a teacher on many journeys, I realized they got such a tickle out of the lessons on the importance of context clues that I expanded the concept of "big" words. One example was an article about a former Governor of Georgia, Lester Maddox, who, in an old article, was pictured, standing in the doorway of a little diner. In the accompanying photo, he was proudly brandishing an ax, while above him was a sign over the entrance, "Whites Only." The caption bore his words that, while he was Governor, the sign would be obeyed. He looked like

evil incarnate; he also looked foolish. Here was a living anach-
ronism in *Time* magazine. The text commenced the tale with,
"The hebetudinous Governor of Georgia . . ." What a word!

We joyfully filled the board with our possible definitions
for "hebetudinous," based on the information we gleaned
from the small story, the picture, and the liberal bent of *Time*.
This was a fine and real example of our abilities to use context clues. What could "hebetudinous" mean? We then
checked the dictionary to see how close we came. "Could
we, in fact, get the gist from our clues? Could we, using our
brains and those clues, be almost as deft as the dictionary?" I
asked rhetorically. We then could, it was conceivable, have
The *Heather Dictionary, The Andrea Dictionary, The Donald
Dictionary*, could we not? Not *just Funk and Wagnall's but John
and Wagnall's* or simply, *Joey's*.

They were enthralled with this "unknown" and "big"
word becoming theirs. They could sneer that the comments
they heard in the hall were obviously spoken by a
hebetudinous fellow. Their irksome brothers and sisters could
now be described with an original twist. Confounding their
peers could be accomplished; for the latter would be dumfounded, hebetudinous, upon hearing the epithet used with
aplomb. Power.

They were pleased that they had "acquired," in their
estimation, a most useful word. It went so well, salt and pep-
per, with a word I had previously put on our descriptive words'
list, "erudite." They were my erudite pupils, and they basked
in the glow of being so called. To be equated with scholars?
Yes, they liked that.

**Most students will rise to expectations and enjoy the
trip.** I treated them as bright, scholarly individuals; and, much
of the time, most learned to conduct themselves as such. "My
erudites." Now they had a word, not only for what they were,
"erudite"; they had a word for what they were not,
"hebetudinous." There was some conjecture about Gover-

35

nor Maddox, however, among the students. They wondered if he would sue *Time*. They decided that a racist, who spewed such a heinous statement, showed that "the Governor was too hebetudinous to know what 'hebetudinous' meant." That made them howl with laughter. They "owned" the word.

Now don't guffaw and say that such words they would never use. It is more of an idea of words, that words are everybody's, that they're not scary. They learned unequivocally that they could figure out word meanings, that some words were fun "to throw around," and that "big words" were no more difficult to use and learn than "regular words." They used them to a fare-thee-well. I would say that they should sing words and dance 'em and draw them and recite them. To own them, they must use them in their speaking and their writing, exaggerating them initially, of course, like showing off a new boyfriend or girlfriend. The vocabulary words from their vocabulary books, the words learned as they read their assigned stories and essays and novels, as well as from lessons and discussions, would be all but useless letters, if not used. The students had to begin to incorporate them, perhaps slowly and exaggeratedly at first, into their own world of words. Then they would no longer be useless; they would be their "property."

They would often try to impress their other teachers with the words they thought would confound them. One teacher reacted in such a negative fashion; he would write on their papers, "Did you learn this from Ms. Tanner?" The students had used their words correctly, but, of course, sounded a bit showy, a bit too scholarly for students, perhaps. I did hope that that teacher would recognize that what he observed was students attempting, in fact, to do what they were often told, "Use your vocabulary in order to learn your words." For instance, describing Albert Einstein as erudite did not, in my estimation, seem "over the top."

What better way is there to learn words? Truly learn them.

Research and our own experience certainly have shown us that memorization alone simply doesn't work—not in any lasting way.

Being alert to such negativity from a teacher is needed. He knew very well that I encouraged students to use their own voices in their work; but we're talking about context clues here, and word parts and pronunciation and confidence and enjoying, actually enjoying, words. I wanted to grab that teacher by the shoulders and with one shake say, "Hey, wake up!" Why did he feel it necessary to criticize the students' work? To demean their efforts? What a shame.

And, ah, "pneumonoultramicroscopicsilicovolcano coneosis," what a tool that was. I don't recall where I stumbled across this very long, but very pronounceable, very definable word. I knew they would love it and that it would help them in our study of context clues and our unit on word parts, structural analysis, if you will. They would beat out its rhythms on the desks, "choo-choo train" style, as I went chugging up and down the aisles; for everyone wanted a turn at proving it could glide off his tongue. How very helpful it was in demonstrating the usefulness of both syllabication and etymology. They enjoyed showing off in front of their parents and friends and feigning a blasé attitude (with their "insider" knowledge) that it was not, contrary to first impressions, the longest word in the English language. It was merely, not so merely to my erudites, a very long, but easy-to-use-and-define word—once you knew how. And knew how they did.

Without a dictionary, we split it. Pneu-mo-no-ul-tra-mi-cro-sco-pic-si-li-co-vol-ca-no-co-ne-o-sis—close enough to begin pronunciation. Hop on that choo-choo. Or beat it out on the desk with a rhythmic cha-cha beat. It's glorious.

Now, separate it into parts, using the dictionary only when you must:

Pneumono=lungs, ultra=very fine, extremely, micro=small, scopic=seeing [so small one needs a microscope to see]

---

silico=silicone, volcano=deep in the earth, osis=disease. Put them all together, they spell mother—oops, different tune. Put them all together, we have a disease of the lungs, caused by inhaling extremely small particles (silicone dust) of silicone, which comes from deep in the earth. What did this all prove? When one has the tools, such as how to utilize syllabication, structural analysis, etymology, context clues, and only as a last resort, the dictionary, one can define and pronounce thousands of words with skill and confidence, not to mention pleasure.

2. SMILE. YOU'RE A PERSON. GRIN, LAUGH, SHARE

At the beginning of a year or of a course, present yourself as the person in charge. Establish the goals and set the procedures, explaining them. This does not mean that you are a robot; you are not plastic man. You have a personality; let it shine. You are quite capable of being firm about setting the climate of the class, while, at the same time, being human.

I guarantee that, if you begin the term or the year as their friend, as the nice and kind teacher who just wants to be one of them, "y'know, working together," you will not "get them back." Many new teachers begin with this sisterly or brotherly attitude. Remember that, in some instances, the teacher is not much older than the students, but those students look to the teacher to set the tone. Remember that you are a professional, highly skilled and trained. Behave like one. You are also a man or a woman who has warmth and sensitivity.

Many young teachers regret that first year, realizing they were never in control. They naively began a routine of making liking one another the primary focus, and the class became either increasingly unruly; or they simply did not pay attention and, consequently, didn't learn very much, or "all of the above." Learn from their mistakes. Begin with a clear seriousness of purpose; you can always "loosen up" later.

Share a joke, tell a story, laugh out loud. Your own individual qualities make you unique. Once you have set the tone of the course, you are entitled to be you. I used to begin the week giving the Tanner movie reviews, or telling about the grand museum I visited, or the great new restaurant I went to, the videos I rented. Then I would ask them to share with me their weekend activities. Slowly they began to open up and discuss their reviews, their jobs, and their pastimes. This give-and-take took less than five minutes. "Hey, Ms. Tanner, what did you think of Brad Pitt's acting?"

3. REMEMBER WHY YOU WENT INTO THIS; HELP THEM

Don't subscribe to the "injection theory" of learning. Learning is developmental. If last year's teacher did, in fact, teach them the rules for the comma—as did other teachers before her—but you find that they still do not know how or when to use the comma consistently, teach them. Don't whine; don't blame the other teacher(s). Refresh the learning. Review. Don't complain that they didn't learn it, or that the previous teachers didn't teach it or teach it well. Learning builds on learning, and now they are one year older, more mature themselves. Ideas clarify sometimes with a little time.

Give them ample opportunities to review. Demonstrate why that particular item is important to learn. (I always thought the comma was a rather remarkable, little piece of punctuation, which one can consistently utilize to make writing clearer.) Drill is not a dirty word. Once they have had a full refresher, hold them responsible for this learning, and, subsequently, each unit of study, throughout the course.

Students respond to structure and review. Don't adhere to the "you-were-taught-this-before-in-a-previous-year-by another-teacher; therefore-you-have been-injected-with-this-knowledge, which-now-you-carry-with-you-forever" theory. It's obviously not true; much of what you do may be review.

1-TANN

The teacher who has them next year may, in fact, wonder if you ever taught them certain items. Try to do your job so well, in so organized a fashion, that next year's teacher can build on the foundation you have laid.

Many students learn when and what they must. If you set the standard low, they simply do not study. If you give the tests, the papers, and hold them responsible throughout the course for what is taught, they, and you, have a chance. If their grades for their work and on the report cards are true reflections of their study and their effort, then they, and you, will succeed. It has to be "As ye sow, so shall ye reap" in order for it (the course) to be meaningful to them.

4. SET AND MAINTAIN PROCEDURES

Right off the bat, establish some ground rules, for example

—One person talks at a time.

—If a student has something to say, he should raise his hand and wait to be called on.

—Speak so everyone can hear.

—Treat everyone with respect.

—Do not get out of the seat without permission.

—Once the student enters the room, he should take a seat.

You will find that they are safer, physically safer, if they are not allowed to roam or stand around, whether in homeroom, in class, or before or after a class. They are young and frisky. You are the supervisor, so supervise. Don't feel that every directive needs to be explained to or approved by them. You are the teacher; you are in charge.

Next door to me one year was a math class, many of whom were howling and racing around the aisles. I looked in disbelief through the glass portion of the door that separated the rooms. The group screaming and cavorting was a class that I had for reading. They were a wonderful class, bright, responsive, and well behaved. The math teacher explained to me later that she let them run around because, once they're through with their work, "they just can't seem to stay in their seats." Do you want to bet?

I welcomed the teacher to observe that class in my room, or any of my classes. They do stay in their seats; they do remain silent when a test or a written exercise is completed, so everyone can finish their work. They do behave well. She was amazed, truly amazed. **Students become what you expect or allow them to become, in most instances.** I expected them to be budding scholars, manifesting enthusiasm about the discussion, the work. She expected them to be rambunctious, little children, so rife with energy that they were incapable of controlling themselves.

She was from the "aren't-they-adorable?" school. Trained as an elementary teacher, an education major, she did not focus primarily on the math. Getting along with them, keeping them in good spirits, that was her emphasis.

5. CREATE AN ATMOSPHERE OF SCHOLARSHIP

The discussion, the routine, the displays, the treatment of individuals—everything should convey that your room is a room of learning. Brimming with books and festooned with their papers and projects, the classroom should exude the aura that in this space there are students, real students, learning. Write each class's homework assignments on a board and keep them current. Put up a bit of inspiration or humor or a quotation by or about someone or something they are studying. Find descriptive lines about the season of the year or ones related to a newsworthy event of the present or the past:

"As crude a weapon as the cave man's club, the chemical barrage has been hurled against the fabric of life."— Rachel Carson (1962)

"Never let the fear of striking out get in your way."—Babe
Ruth

"Oh, to be in England now that April's there . . ."—Robert
Browning

"Power is not a means; it is an end."—George Orwell

"Four be the things I'd been better without: Love, curiosity,
freckles, and doubt."—Dorothy Parker

6. TEACH ABOUT AND REINFORCE A CLIMATE OF RESPECT

Discussions of readings and current happenings—all discussions—must be demonstrations of respect for one another
and for the ideas of everyone. When someone expresses a
view that is contrary or unpopular, remind students of two
things you have repeatedly stated, right from the beginning,
namely, that ideas and comments must be phrased intelligently and responded to in a like manner. In such an atmosphere, students will gradually be unafraid to express their
opinions; and all sides of an issue can be heard.

In a discussion of Shakespeare's sonnets, homosexuality
became a topic. A teacher must continually reinforce the concept of free discussion; for, in an atmosphere of polite discourse, all subjects, even controversial ones, can be exam-
ined and illuminated. Students are entitled to express and
hear differing viewpoints, as long as the discussion abides
"by the rules." Those rules are the very same ones that you
should, from time to time, remind them of and the very same
ones with which you began the year or the course. Therefore, there is nothing unusual about the discussion when the
subject is a heated issue.

During our poetry unit, a Millay poem sparked a discussion of women's changing role and the impact of tradition.
The topic was the term, "Ms." Some of the boys in the class
found this term "pushy" and "silly." Several of them, raising
their hands to speak, of course, expressed the idea that the

term was unnecessary. I went to the board and wrote the terms for men: "Mr." Whoops, it's not "terms," at all; it's "term." All men have the designation of "Mr." For women, society has handed down the tradition of separate terms, one for the unmarried, another for the married. Why?

Why does a woman not only change her last name upon marriage, but "lose" her first, as well? Let's just examine this. And on and on went the ideas, the discussion. A wedding invitation, even today, will read, "Mr. and Mrs. Theodore Smith invite you to attend . . ." Poor Mrs. Smith. She doesn't even have a first name. I relate that both friends and relatives contend that society dictates that this form is "the correct one." "Correct" by whose standards? And who is this person, this thing called "society?" Could not the invitation read, "Sally and Theodore Smith?" A spirited give-and-take ensued. And they were thinking.

I wanted the class merely to try to brush away some preconceived notions, to question "tradition." As ever, they were free to choose their own course, but they had to read, to discuss, to think. Thus we returned to Robert Frost's poem, "Mending Wall" and to the neighbor so intent to rebuild the stone wall because he was brought up to believe in the tradition that "good fences make good neighbors." And return we did in order to discuss whether fences actually "make good neighbors." We spoke of various traditions and the concept of tradition itself. It was a lively and interesting exchange of ideas, examining beliefs and customs, using our poems as the catalysts.

When I receive an invitation, I shared with them, written in the traditional way (Mr. and Mrs. Timothy Lake), I am dumfounded. People tell me that the owners of the invitation businesses state that this is the "acceptable way, the way that society dictates." Who says? I have asked my classes to use "fresh thinking," to start from scratch, so to speak, to understand how some of our traditions began, for example, and then, sweeping away proscribed notions, to choose what is "acceptable," to empower themselves to know that they are society.

Perhaps, some traditions should be altered, some dropped, and some revered and held tightly to our bosom. But, wouldn't it be illuminating –and fun—to examine their origins? The choice then becomes the students', as well as ours; but they, and we, should realize that, indeed, there is a choice. I was bemused to note that some young women today selected the traditional way, unaware and, maybe, unconcerned that they had a choice at all. (The poor dears have no first names, at all. Maybe, once married, they didn't need them anymore.)

So I shared my views, and they shared theirs. It was a lesson connected to the ideas in our poetry, but it was also a lesson in how differing opinions can be exchanged with respect shown to all participants. The students had done the readings, so they were prepared. Furthermore, the students followed the guidelines of the class, which were to allow each person to speak without interruption; to raise their hands to be recognized; to phrase their comments or questions in a respectful way; to use, where possible, facts to substantiate their statements; and to treat everyone with dignity. Also, it was hoped that they could learn to hold up to the light, rather than swallow whole, entrenched ideas and traditions, to think about them, to actually stop and think about them.

There are classrooms in which students call out to whoever has entered, a student delivering a notice, a teacher dropping off a book; and sometimes this is accompanied by hooting and name calling. This, of course, makes students reluctant to enter those teachers' classes again. The inappropriate behavior is just a continuation of what had been going on in that classroom. The students obviously were yelling out and being insolent before any visitor ever entered. What type of atmosphere would exist for an intelligent and respectful discussion in such a room? Some teachers have encouraged this rather loose, "hangin' out" type of setting, mistaking this for a communal, democratic ambience. Some have simply let the beginnings of unacceptable behavior escalate.

A teacher must, at all times, create an atmosphere that obviates any misunderstanding about what is acceptable behavior. Students who then know they will be treated with dignity and fairness will be encouraged to express their ideas and, concomitantly, will treat their fellow classmates in the same fashion.

Part of any discussion, of learning, is listening. It is absorbing what another is stating; therefore, students, it follows, must be allowed the quiet to voice their ideas, while others listen in silence—blessed silence.

I have been invited to participate in discussions with the principal and a student in which a student, upon being sent to the office by a teacher for misbehaving, tells the principal that the teacher didn't show him respect. Well-trained, experienced administrators see through this immediately. The student rants that he "just didn't feel like sitting down" when the teacher instructed him to do so (how dare she!). "She coulda waited. What's the big deal?" (Don'tcha love it?)

A teacher must remove students from the class who disrupt the learning process and those who act in a disrespectful or rude fashion. Remember that you set the rules, you explained them, and you gave reminders. Now, both you—and the administrators—must reinforce them each and every day in order that they become de rigueur.

7. YOUR GOALS, AND THOSE OF THE ADMINIS-TRATION, THOUGH SIMILAR, ARE NOT THE SAME

What's your main goal? C'mon, I want to see if you're catching on.

Your main goal is to help students learn the subject, improve in many ways in the subject that you are teaching. What you have to do is ensure that everything is in place to accomplish that goal—everything that you can control, that is, such as the atmosphere, the discipline, the proper materials, your attitude and enthusiasm, your organizational skills, etc.

The administration's main goal, in many instances, is one of public relations and keeping down costs. Of course, administrators want students to learn. Of course, they want the students to thrive, as you do. Of course, they want you to be effective in your work and content with your job. Their primary objective in today's world, however, is "keeping a good face," maintaining the aura of well-being. This is oftimes accomplished through evasion and obfuscation and, occasionally, through intimidation.

Ralph Waldo Emerson said, "Big jobs usually go to men who prove their ability to outgrow small ones." He certainly would change his mind if he could observe today's schools. Too many administrators are simply not educational leaders. How could they be when many were not good teachers? Those in the position to hire misconstrue organizational skills or popularity or, perhaps, toughness, with the ability to create an atmosphere of scholarship for the students and support for the faculty. There are too many principals and assistant principals who were chosen as a reward for years of service; some were considered affable and articulate; some were assistant principals and were moved up to the next wrung with "the devil you know . . ." kind of philosophy, promulgated by school committees. Too often they choose people who "mean well," which is such a tepid recommendation in a profession that cries out for scholarship, for leadership, for expertise.

The following is a brief list of some of my administrators:

—My first principal had vision in planning, but his overriding goal was to avoid any conflict. His constant reminder to the faculty was "The best way to solve a problem is to avoid it altogether."

—This assistant junior high principal was soft-spoken, well liked (as a former teacher in the same building), and wanted to remain unaware of what was going on so that he wouldn't have to take any action. He made no impact, which was exactly what he wanted.

—Brought in because he had a reputation for being tough as an assistant principal, this administrator was aware of everything in the building, in every class. He knew who were the effective teachers and who were simply not doing their jobs. Especially hard on the meek teachers, he intentionally intimidated them. All his former teachers would agree that, although he was undeniably a martinet, gruff, and devoid of sophistication, on the whole, he supported his faculty and demanded the rules be followed not only by the students, but also by all his teachers. Thus, he trained many teachers well; and, due in large measure to his tutelage, his educators continued in other grades or other schools, still maintaining tight discipline, good organization, and solid teaching.

—There was a team of a principal and an assistant who worked well together, but was not well liked by the faculty. The former was a good leader, I thought, bright and well read. His flaw was his attention to public relations, another contest, another party, another assembly, and another photo in the local paper. The teachers used to sing about him, "Hello, it's me. My name is Pinky Lee," due to the emphasis he placed on performances. Me? I agreed that there were too many of these; but, if the superintendent had been doing his job of leadership, the principal would have been curbed a bit, for he had admirable qualities. He was warm, intelligent, and understood and tried to encourage the quest for excellence.

Pinky Lee's assistant was a seasoned vice principal, who had the demeanor of a military man and had been an inspirational football coach. He was a competent disciplinarian, who walked that fragile tightrope of being both liked and feared by the students, being consistent and experienced. This combination is vital in an administrator in charge of the building's discipline. He went by the rules; and students, then and now, understood and needed that structure. The students—and I—agreed that he was an educator in charge of situations, the embodiment of "firm but fair."

(May I add that the "gruff" principal mentioned previously also trained him. They, too, made an interesting tandem; for, under their combined supervision, both students and faculty knew where they stood.) They shared a flaw, that of being too rigid and unaccommodating of, and, on occasion, downright hostile to soft-spoken, mild-mannered, gentle male faculty members. To them, these were qualities of weakness. One got the idea that they both felt these traits were not fit for teachers and certainly not for male teachers.

—A principal who also had a stint as an assistant principal and had "done himself proud" in that position was one of my favorite administrators. He roamed the building, popped into classes unannounced, and greeted everyone with cordiality. He was a sweet man, respectful and polite to all, students, teachers, and parents. His grace could be counted on, for he conducted himself with a sense of style and class. We enjoyed that he exuded warmth and humor and a desire to improve himself. He was one of those people who learned a word a day and hurled it into every sentence and situation. Doing one's homework would obviate problems on a test, and calling a parent would obviate later concerns. How commendable.

A TEACHER'S MANUAL

A lover of scholarship, he admired those who had command of the language and would create his own vocabulary words.

Students who were snickering, as he was advising them about their misdeeds, were told sternly that they should immediately cease being so frejovious. They were warned that their frejoviousness would get them in even more trouble if it continued. I loved this. He carved out both an adjective and a noun—and the students clearly understood what he meant.

He was amiable with a whiff of the officious, perhaps. Some of his former fellow teachers resented him; I thought he was grand and rather "presidential." He carried himself as a leader and was open to ideas that fostered scholarship. The school ran well, for he was alert, aware, and organized. He supported his faculty; and he supported his students, as well.

Students knew that they would be dealt with fairly in a no-nonsense fashion, no coddling by this principal for anyone who disrupted learning. This was a man comfortable in his role, comfortable enough to be amiable and charming on the one hand and stern and just on the other—when needed.

—Another high school principal followed, an affable fellow, who was knowledgeable of his role and so looked and sounded like perfect casting as a secondary school principal, but chose not to fulfill those expectations. He charmed students and faculty; he was engaging. He gave the impression, true, I believe, that if he wanted, he could be an administrative leader. He simply didn't "want." Vision meant work; department meetings and faculty meetings meant issues raised, problems to fix. No meetings, or few meetings, meant fewer problems; therefore, "that was the way it was."

He had the background and the demeanor to make an impact; and, when he chose to step in, he was highly capable of swift and sound action. Most times, however, he chose not to. He evidently wanted that calm sea we dream of, like the

49

-TANN

soft sound of the water, lapping gently against the boat of life. The difference, perhaps, is that we don't usually associate this dream fantasy with our jobs. And who would expect this serenity within a high school setting? Yet the man with so much potential made the choice not to fulfill it. He was intelligent, charming, attractive, and responsive; he simply was not interested in motivating a staff.

Let me share some "war stories."

"Please take your seat," said the health teacher to the high school girl. She stood in the aisle, ignoring the bell that signified the start of the period and the direction from the instructor that everyone should be seated. She continued to talk and stand, and the teacher repeated his directive. Again she paid him no mind. Again he repeated himself. She then yelled that she didn't like the location of her seat, and she wasn't going to sit in it. Mr. Health cautioned the student several more times (which, in part, is probably why students behave in this fashion—several more times?) because there was an intimidation by the administrators imbedded in many teachers' minds, the spoken and unspoken "rule" not to send students to the office.

You were to "handle the problems yourself," or teachers, at least some of them, feared they would be thought of as weak. A seasoned and confident teacher would have ignored that type of admonition, realizing that allowing insubordination, allowing the disruption of learning, cannot be condoned and certainly not encouraged.

This continued, in spite of the teacher telling the girl that her seat problem would be addressed after class. Determined to get her own way, she then wound an elastic band around her finger, angry that she now, in fact, was sitting in the unwelcome seat. She pulled the elastic tightly and created indentations in the skin of her finger, screaming out that she wanted the nurse to look at her "wound." He refused to comply and continued on with the lesson, as she, undaunted, kept up her pleas about her bruised finger. Mr. Health and others were so intimidated by and so eager to avoid any confrontation with the administrators that they rarely sent these objectionable students from the class.

Finally the girl said, "I'm going to the nurse, whether you like it or not." He told her to be quiet and remain seated. She stood and stomped down the aisle, yelling, "Fuck you." She then slammed out of the room.

The assistant principal felt it necessary, after listening to the girl and then hearing from the teacher, to have them both in his office together to tell their "versions" again. Because the offensive language was not said directly to the teacher's face, as recounted by the student, the assistant principal could not, he contended, suspend the girl. Now if the language had, indeed, been uttered to his face, the health teacher was assured that the punishment (one hour of after-school detention) would have been more severe. Sure, sure, sure.

Such mishandling of situations demoralizes staff members and encourages insolence in other students.

Students caught smoking marijuana in the boys' room were suspended for five days. The assistant principal (not the same one as above) embraced them by the shoulders and shook their hands, as they were leaving the building. He, smiling, told them to enjoy their days off and to have a good time.

A substitute teacher, who "taught" every day, ignored the lesson plans left by absent teachers because he said that he preferred to talk to the students for the period and that he felt inadequate to teach English or history or math, etc. The students would be running around the room, or smacking one another, or racing in the corridor, or just yelling. No teaching went on; no learning took place. They could relax and not have to do anything, which many, of course, enjoyed. Some liked to chat and joke with the "nice man," who treated them cordially and engaged them in animated conversation. In all probability, although the reasons he proffered were valid, the main reason that he did not give the lesson plan a try is that it is a difficult task to be a teacher and often a grueling task to be a substitute.

Teaching is difficult. I think of it as both an art and a craft. Numerous days it's like that sensation when I hear Andrea Bocelli sing "Con Te Partiro" (no kidding). Often it's akin to the feeling that I get right through to my bones of a wondrous experience, like a March Madness team smoothly executing a fast break; or the elation from a Broadway show—that's what teaching, more often than not, felt like to me. Did you ever go to Fenway Park on a beautiful summer day, and rise to sing "The National Anthem," and look around at the green field and the eager ballplayers and realize how lucky you were to be there? Most days, that's how teaching felt to me. Teaching is complex; and, as in many things, when all "the cylinders are clickin'," this difficult vocation is rife with inspiration for both the teacher and the students.

Substitutes must teach a lesson, not merely baby-sit; they must exert their authority. Therefore, administrators must support efforts to control a class and to teach a lesson. Although teachers, in general, are relatively poorly remunerated, and substitutes are, as well, (it might be considered adequate compensation for baby-sitting), just watching over students is not enough. They should be learning, as well as behaving; and no one has the right to give students license to behave poorly.

The administrators made a special point of praising the full-time substitute teacher and other substitutes who "taught" in a like fashion; for they were at their positions every day; and "the students liked them." Getting and keeping substitutes is a daunting task; and administrators are so grateful when they have reliable, educated, decent people to fill in. If, however, the administrators had someone train the subs, if they do not want to do it themselves, and then backed up the poor, picked-upon subs, the students would soon get the message that they must do the work; and they must behave.

Study halls still exist. They may have euphemistic titles at times, like "Directed Study"; but what they are, in fact, are large blocks of time with many students having no place to go. There are not enough teachers in the building to accommodate all the courses that should be offered, and there are not enough teachers because there is not enough money to hire them. One might say that, arguably, the funds went elsewhere, i.e. special education or professional development or public relations efforts or more computers. One might also add that there is simply not enough money to do all that should be done and do it well—but that is a secret. Sh.

As an example, both Greek and Latin were recently offered in a small school that could have utilized these funds, offering courses that more students could take advantage of. I have nothing against classical languages. These were instituted, however, with no thought to priorities, which, consequently, led to large study halls in the cafeteria for students who had no courses to elect.

In these study halls, which were often supervised by inexperienced and ineffectual teachers, the discipline became so bad that students were allowed by the administration to listen via earphones to radios and CD players and, for all I know, TV's. This, not too long ago, would have been anathema. Students who should be doing their homework or reading, if, in fact, they must be relegated to study hall, listening to rap music or nodding off in school? (What did you think they were listening to, Mozart?) They were allowed to play with their Gameboys, play cards, listen to the radio or tapes and CD's in school because the teachers and administrators couldn't control the situation. Focus on this scenario because it tells a great deal in a succinct fashion about school today. This is an academic atmosphere?

"Directed Study" is the term originally used for courses

taken by individual students who require more depth in an offering. Hence, a student who is very bright and who has, perhaps, taken all the electives that she needs and wants, chooses to take a quarter-course in, say, Emily Dickinson's poetry. A teacher "directs" what she is to read, research, and accomplish on her own. The student meets with the teacher periodically to discuss the student's ideas and examine the student's work. Essentially, the student is on her own, but under the direction of the teacher.

This is a fine offering for a gifted student. However, to use the term to designate study halls with 90, 100, or more students, and then to further exacerbate the situation by allowing students not to study is, indeed, a paradox.

8. PLAN IN UNITS OF STUDY

Experiencing the many connections in learning makes the subject easier for the students to learn and more interesting. An example would by "my" Edgar Allen Poe unit, which developed over a period of years. One goal of the unit was to learn about the life and the work of Mr. Poe and investigate how the one may have influenced the other. Another objective was to learn, by using Poe's poems, the techniques and the terminology of poetry and of writing. Learning about outlining, utilizing the events in Poe's life, was another objective of the unit. And, for good measure, we had exercises in listening comprehension, vocabulary, reading comprehension, oral reading, and creative writing, as well.

It was simply a delightful unit. They loved it and became mini experts on, not only Poe, but also the poetic techniques. They enthusiastically beat out the rhymes and rhythms of *The Bells* and got their tongues and minds around the variety of language Poe mastered. They could find with ease the similes, the metaphors, the alliterations, etc.—and understand them. Reveling in the macabre and the artistry, they appreciated "The Tell-Tale Heart" and found "The Cask of Amontillado" delicious, no pun intended.

They took to the outline form, realizing that it aided them in organizing the facts and helped them to distinguish the major from the minor details. As a tool for studying, for learning information, they concluded that the outline was a valuable assistant.

Discussing "Annabel Lee" or "Alone" or even *The Raven*, became a rich learning experience; for they related the sad events in the writer's life to the tone, the choice of language, the subject matter, and the techniques (imagery, for one example) in his work. They empathized, as they soaked up and came to understand Poe's madness and his genius.

We concluded the unit, which contained a variety of measuring tools (comprehension tests, oral discussion, poetry and writing analysis, outlining assignments, etc), with a project on Poe. The project had many options, all of which had the requirement of containing original writing, such as posters, poetry, acting out a play based on the writer's life and/or his work, a short biography, a one-man show (or one woman, as the case may be). In other words, everyone had to do something creative. We dressed up; we had refreshments; and we commiserated on Poe's disappointments. We recited Poe's work, and we attempted to create our own poetry that would mirror our own lives.

I had a marvelous time and was thrilled with their knowledge acquisition and their zest and creativity. The capper was they learned, learned well; and they appreciated, too. Now, you could ask, "All of them?" Maybe not. But most truly enjoyed the experience, and the others must have been great fakers.

9. BE FLEXIBLE, CHANGING A LESSON PLAN, A ROUTINE—ON OCCASION

Spontaneity ignites a class sometimes. A discussion, a

comment, a lesson may take on a different light, or zoom off in a different direction, or may infuse students with an energy, a challenge, an enthusiasm that you had not predicted. Go with it.

A lesson on vocabulary was focused on diacritical marks. The students had not mastered their usage; many had never had a lesson on them at all. They so "took to them." I encouraged them to use the dictionary, make it their tool, to enable them to pronounce any word. They enjoyed being able to mark words themselves and to show off their ability to unlock heretofore "hard words." A word like "schism" they could deftly mark and pronounce correctly as "sism." They enjoyed the mastering of a life skill; they "got a kick out of it." Had I planned that it would take the whole period? No. Was it worthwhile, as they challenged one another over and over again? Yes.

A lesson went "off-track," as a girl who was usually rather reticent, got animated about the treatment of athletes. We had been discussing a story (which was not about athletes), and she got " involved" with one of the characters. Rather than make short shrift of this, I called upon others, as well, to voice their reactions to her comments. She was articulate, engaging, and intelligent in her recounting her anecdotal references. The class was energized into telling their stories, too. It was wonderful to let the sparks of spontaneity brighten the room. This was not the lesson's objective—and it was wonderful.

Change the seating arrangements every term or every month. Let them view the class and their classmates from a fresh perspective. Change the bulletin board displays. Put life in the room.

"I know we usually do our vocabulary review on Thursdays; but today, for half of the period, let's examine these magazines and newspapers I brought in to see if, in fact, any of them use any of "our words" or any interesting vocabulary, for that matter. Then let's discuss whether you are incorporating them in your own speech and your written work. Do you ever use them at home around the dinner table, for example? Raise your hands and share with us some of your examples, please." Just the alteration of the day's plan got them.

10. RECOGNIZE VARIOUS LEARNING STYLES, AS WELL AS ABILITIES—

A unit should allow, when possible, for a variety of approaches. Some teachers almost always lecture; some give notes every day; and some lean too frequently on group learning (buzz groups). There are classes when listening skills should be utilized, and there are lessons that lend themselves to discussion. Often, the board should be used as a learning tool, visualization. On occasion, the students going to the board to put on their examples, their answers, or analyses, changes the routine and invigorates the class. Music and audiotapes are sometimes useful for illustration, for enrichment, or for a change in the routine. The point is that all inclinations, all learning styles should be tapped.

Writing is a skill that I had them use almost every day, whether in class or for homework; for the drill gave them increasing proficiency with expression, as well as serving as a review of their grammar skills. Many skills should be called upon, and a teacher soon recognizes that certain students are articulate orally, but find written expression difficult. Some students rarely exercised their abilities with oral discussion in the past, thereby never getting an opportunity to improve them. Call on them; help them. Don't allow them to slide through. How does one improve without practice? That's rhetorical, folks.

You'll find students who have fine visual and/or auditory memory. Commend them and give them credit for what they can do and try to help them develop increased skill in what they can't.

11. CALL ON EVERY STUDENT

Let them know that their enthusiasm, their participation will influence your grading. Hear everyone's voice almost every day. Call on them to answer a question, to pose a question, or make a statement. Do not let the phrase, "I don't know" get them off the hook; some of them have been allowed to stay in a cave of silence for years due to their lack of confidence, their diffidence, or the more vocal and exuberant students getting the attention. Say aloud that you value their reactions and that you believe responding to the homework is helpful. Tell them that you want to hear their voices and that the way to learn to respond orally, as in writing, is to get lots of practice.

"Jeffrey, that was an interesting comment you wrote on the homework. Tell the class what you found out, please."

"We haven't heard from you today, Bonnie; what did you think of Liz's statement?"

"Well, what did you think of that, Casey?"

12. ENCOURAGE RESPONDING WITH CORRECT USAGE, FULL SENTENTENCES—NOT SLANG, NOT, "WHATEVER"

They quickly learn what each teacher is about, meaning what you expect of them. Stop the routine to make it clear that an answer, such as, "That story sucked." is not acceptable. Explain why it is not the way to respond and elucidate, giving some suggestions, as to how intelligent people converse with one another. They will learn quickly.

Often I have observed classes in which an experienced teacher (rookies all do it) accepts, without comment, a response from a student that is too softly or too rapidly spoken, or, perhaps, so succinct or mumbled, and fails to correct the student. Remarks are not just the purview of the teacher. They are to be shared by the entire class and spoken loudly enough and clearly enough for the class to hear and understand. This is a time to stop and ask the student to repeat the remark (with some further direction, i.e. "Would you speak up, please?" or, "Would you put that in a sentence, so that the class can understand what you are saying?" or, "Whoa, slow down. Class, we have to remember that there is a need to be heard and understood by the whole group. Now, please, try again."

What is the sense of teaching grammar if, in fact, you do not insist on good grammar in both their writing, as well as their speaking? Remember in this, as in everything on the job, you are the role model. They may try to emulate you in your maxims, in your speech, or in your conduct. If you, and draw their attention to the fact you do, speak loudly, slowly, clearly—and well—they will take notice.

Remind them of the judgment of strangers. People react to our actions, our attitude, our attire, and our speech. Strangers snap to judgment instantly, based on what they see and hear, which, fair or unfair, is a quick way to evaluate someone. "What is in our guts," I used to tell my students, "no one knows." Therefore, we should look enthusiastic, alert, and friendly. You may be thinking, "Oy vey, that Ms. Tanner is going on and on and on." But if your appearance or demeanor doesn't give it away, I'll never know.

Your voice and your wording are wrapped up in your attitude. They should try to sound like what you are—or certainly can be, intelligent, interesting, and interested. "All the time?" they may whine. Why not? Won't a teacher be more inclined to give you that extra point if she has a good impression of you? Wouldn't your teacher write a glowing recommendation for one who not only worked and studied, but spoke well and was pleasant? Wouldn't a boss hire you with that behavior? Wouldn't you impress a college registrar? A coach? A girlfriend? That is the same disposition teachers should insist on in a classroom setting, as well. **Speaking and behaving intelligently are daily class requirements.**

13. EXCHANGE IDEAS WITH YOUR COLLEAGUES

Talk about plans that work and lessons that don't. A successful plan of another teacher may be duplicated or modified for your class. It's fun and interesting, too, to hear the array of creativity. One faculty member may have the book you were looking for, or you may spread those wonderfully original projects on the teachers' room table to share with them. This communication evokes an openness that is healthy and communal. It may lead to after-school coffee or a combined field trip or a new friendship. Tips on methods and materials can lead only to improved teaching. A colleague had the students write letters to themselves, which he saved to mail to them in five or ten years. He used it for a multiplicity of purposes—or I added some: how to write a friendly letter, grammar reinforcement, the use of adjectives, etc. It was a clever plan, and I asked if I could "borrow."

14. TALK TO GUIDANCE COUNSELORS AND FELLOW TEACHERS TO LEARN MORE ABOUT YOUR STUDENTS

Guidance counselors, good ones, can be such assets to a school. They are compassionate, yet sensible, and help a student see the reality of his personal situation. Some, regrettably, are just ill suited to the job or the age level; and there is little administrative supervision to identify those counselors who are ineffective, disorganized, or downright inept.

One agreed with great enthusiasm to write a senior recommendation for a student and then proceeded with such a detailed and bleak one, based mainly on a couple of old records in his folder, that no school would have ever taken a chance on the boy. She could have demurred, saying that she hadn't known him very long, which was true, or that she felt that she could not give the type of recommendation he wanted. Students deal with truth much better than with deception. Don't we all? Had she been suited for her position she would have recommended the student, who is a fine boy, talented and personable. It is true that he had problems (many do) and was not the hardest working of young men. None of this should have excluded him from a hopeful recommendation.

A student was removed from a class for being insubordinate and for screaming, "Fuck you, you bitch," when told by the chemistry teacher to open his book (for the third time); or he would be sent to the office. The guidance counselor greeted him with a sheepish grin and a "Now, honey, what did you do?" said in a softly sweet tone. This welcome was followed by a meeting that went something like this:

"Now, Ms. Teacher, Karen says that you don't respect her and that is why she insulted you and slammed out of your room. What do say to that?" Inadequately trained counselors did, in fact, deal with such situations in this manner. And that was not, by any means the only time or the only counselor.

Let us, indeed, not put teachers in this type of defensive position, student advocate or no student advocate. All teachers are student advocates, not just guidance counselors—or they should be.

Counselors, I have seen it a hundred, maybe a thousand times, can be sources of calm, of privacy, of support, as well as liaisons between the students and their teachers, and, often, between the students and their parents. They learn about the teachers and can match up with precision a teacher and a child in need. Some guidance counselors are miracle workers with an innate sense of understanding. When this is accompanied by experience and maturity, counselors are valuable resources for not just students, but teachers, as well.

I have dealt with several who are efficient, effective, caring; they are gems in creating a team approach with the teacher and the student, and, in many instances, the parent, as well.

Today, counselors have so much paperwork and give so much assistance in testing, that they do not have enough time to devote to talking with the students. They, like many teachers, have too much of a workload.

Communicating with colleagues is often illuminating; for you learn about them, as well as the students. Some can throw light on a student's skills in another discipline. Jason, for example, who is fumbling in one subject, is a star in another. Katie, you learn, is a soccer player, who also works part-time and cares for her baby sister. No wonder her work is mediocre. Some information you discern from the students themselves and their work, some from the counselors or the parents; and some of your fellow teachers can help you flesh out more of a total picture.

Be aware, however, not to let others form you opinion for you or allow a student's past to replace your own day-to-day observations and your own dealings with him. Mr. Social Studies, who did not get along with several students each and every class, each and every year, always rushed up to tell me the worst about students; he wanted to "enlighten" me, to help me, he said. Those same "terrible, little boys" were, more often than not, just wonderful in my classes.

Mr. Officious Science, on the other hand, a most pleasant fellow, would relate, reveling in being the purveyor of the tales, class incidents that made me gasp. When he was questioned as to who it was, for example, that shoved the teacher against the wall, or who slammed out of the room and then the school, he would demur. Ah, yes, he would, rather puckishly, convey that he did not want to reveal the student's name. He gave the impression that he wanted to protect the student's identity or that he was unclear as to whether the administration would "allow" him to share this information.

Incidents should be shared. Lord knows we are told often enough "we are a family." The members of the family should be aware of what is going on in the "home." I had been a colleague of Mr. Science for over twenty-five years. He told me countless times about how he respected and admired me, yet I was treated like a stranger by him in certain instances. When most information is not communicated information, it makes what is doled out mere gossip.

We share the students and should not be regarded as the enemy. The administration sets this tone. Thankfully, some principals believe that we constitute a team and make communication a priority; some, to the contrary, believe that "leaking" information gets out to the parents and the community. Tsk. Principals and assistant principals are concerned that parents, upon learning of troubling incidents, will think less of the school. It's that rah-rah-sis-boom-bah mentality. Positive public relations are, to too many school leaders, their number one focus.

A boy shoved a teacher against the wall upon being told to take his seat. He swore, rushed toward the door, pushing her hard on his way out. Couldn't "the community" handle that? Wouldn't it be an informational benefit for all to know that, when such behavior occurs, it is dealt with firmly and fairly? That the teacher was feeling all right? Hiding the normality of school life seems doctrinaire, unethical—and useless.

15. ENLIST PARENTS AS PARTNERS

Most parents are wonderfully cooperative and appreciate a call about their children's progress, work, and behavior. They like being informed and kept up-to-date. Occasionally, there is the parental call that goes something like this:

Parent: I was most upset about my daughter's grade.

Teacher: I would think you would be. But it certainly came as no surprise, since mid-term reports were sent home, and her lack of study was noted. You also ask to see her papers and tests that are given each week, I would assume; so you would have been aware of the quality of her work.

Parent: Do you like my daughter? She says that maybe her grade was so low because you don't like her.

Teacher: Now, sir, may I assure you that I find your daughter to be a nice, young lady. The quality of her work is what we are discussing. She finds the work difficult, has a part-time job, and is very active in extra-curricula activities. Frankly, what I said to her several times is what I now repeat to you. In order to do well in this class, she must study. I realize that it may sound too simplistic to you, but it is that simple. She has missed handing in some homework, done very superficial work on some of her papers, and failed some tests. I appreciate your concern, which I share, I might add. Please encourage her, as I have done, that she certainly can raise this grade and improve her performance.

The parent was not happy with me. He wanted me to kowtow, to intimidate me. I have found it best to be candid and attempt to make parents realize that it is they who should be monitoring the grades, the homework, especially of those canny upperclassmen. I also make it known to them that I was and am available to speak to them after school any time, or that they should send me a note; and I would respond. Today we would, perhaps, do some of this through e-mail.

Picture this scenario. Two mothers, who are friends, ganged up on a young teacher, intimidating her because their sons received low grades on their projects. They came to school irate and downright belligerent. It was obvious to the teacher that, although hints of the students' abilities were contained within the projects, the boys simply waited too long to do all the work they needed; and they had worked too little. They both began their work during the last couple of days of their three-week assignment. The boys knew it; the teacher knew it.

Both parents were demanding, rude, and insulting to this

young woman. They insisted that the grades be changed and that "kinder eyes" view the project, as well. The administrators lent tepid support to the teacher but also gave credence to the charges that the teacher was unfair and, perhaps, a bit too inexperienced to grade the wondrous work fairly. They did this by agreeing to meet with the parents several times; by meeting with the teacher too many times (giving the impression of support, of course); and by allowing the parents to meet, again and again, with the teacher, who was getting very worn down by now.

The teacher did, in fact, raise the marks of both boys, feeling she saved face because she just raised them one grade. She learned her lesson, however, and felt cowed. Flunking bright students with obnoxious parents will not, I suspect, happen again in her career. Perhaps, with some additional experience, she will be able to stand her ground.

Most parents appreciate you, support you, and are grateful for any information about their children's attitude in class, quality of work, and attention to homework and study. Enlist their assistance on the road to their children's improvement to make sure, from time to time, that the homework is completed and that the attitude in class is one of which they would approve. A child who is belligerent in the home will be the same in some, if not all, classes. Some students who are very well behaved in the home are not always so in a class. The parents should be made aware.

Parents should be motivated to ask, around the supper table, "So, how was school today?" And no shrugs or mumbles or non-answers allowed. Convey that parents should expect to hear a bit (Hear that? A bit) of what happened in school. What was discussed in science? What did they do in English? How was the Spanish class today? The student doesn't have to discuss every class or every lesson; but what was going on, in his words, may tell something of his attitude, the class's behavior, the subjects discussed, the assignments, or a teacher's presentation.

Don't let a child dictate that he doesn't wish to recapitulate his day. Tough-o. Parents should relate that it is interesting to hear about the school day. Communicate to parents that they should be informed—in a brief way—of what goes on in classes, in the cafeteria, the labs, and the gym. Period. They are the parents. Several parents have told me that their children "don't like it" when they're asked about their school day. Hey? Who're the parents around here?

"They get surly," one parent confided to me. Another snickered that he gave up asking his son about school because the child always said nothing happened, or that school was boring, or he just shrugged away the queries. What do you think that boy is like in some of his classes?

These are young people who need parental guidance, not just generosity of spirit and funds. Parents need to articulate what type of behavior they expect. Teachers have to do the same.

Parents have the right, if not the obligation, to learn about the teachers and the work and the classroom decorum. I welcomed parents who wanted to sit in and observe and participate in a class.

In a neighboring town, however, a parent sat in a class, clipboard in hand, scowl on face, writing continually with great energy (and wanting the teacher to be aware that she was doing so) what was going on in the room. No, no, no. A parent should be a student for that period. Sit, observe, and, perhaps, participate. You do not, or should not, attempt to do a parent's job; a parent should not try to do yours. Auditing a class is a courtesy, a learning experience.

Observing the classroom itself can render a great deal of information to a parent or administrator. If regularly there are candy, food, or gum wrappers in abundance strewn on the floor, if the desks are freshly gouged or scribbled upon, if papers are scattered on the floor and about the room, something is amiss. This is usually the ambience of a classroom of a teacher who does not have good control.

Many parents became my pals, my friends; and most were so supportive and appreciative of all of the teachers' work and concern for their children. Often, I felt they were like my rooting section, "Go, Tanner, go!"

16. YOU ARE NOT HITLER; ATTILA, THE HUN; OR A MARINE DRILL SERGEANT—DO NOT YELL

I have a strong voice; I make myself heard. I ask that students do the same. But I do not yell. In the cafeteria, so 150 students can, in fact, hear the instructions, it might be necessary to raise one's voice. But to walk down a hall and hear a teacher in a class, screaming, losing his temper, and letting the anger fly fills me with frustration. That same teacher had options: stop, take a deep breath, and deal with the situation; or stop, take a deep breath, and send the student who disrupted the lesson (and probably not for the first time) to the office. The teacher could have stepped right outside the room with the student and spoken to him (this has a short shelf life as an option—use it once with a student. The next time, to the office he goes, and his parents get a call.)

If a teacher has allowed unacceptable behavior in class by ignoring it or by threatening removal from class, but not following through, that behavior becomes like a vine, growing thicker and stronger each day, until it takes over. That teacher should not be surprised that he is driven to distraction, so angry that he finds himself screaming at the perpetrator, or, at times, at the whole class. The students share with each other that "he just lost it."

Some teachers are intimidated, having picked up the message, delivered tacitly or openly by the administrators, that, if you send students to the office for discipline, you show yourself as weak, unable to do your job. Pity the poor new teacher. This is the current message that too many school leaders give in instructions and by their own actions. If a teacher sends a student to the office for swearing, and that student is back at her door within minutes, or if that student receives no disciplinary action, not only is the message clear, the message takes wing and flies all over the building.

A teacher yelling in class is a sign that something is seriously wrong. Stop. You are screaming at a young person in your charge; and everyone else in the room is catching the jolts, as well. Do not be intimidated by previous inaction by the office. Do not be put off by the mandate, delivered at a faculty meeting that teachers should learn to "handle their own problems" or that the office is "too busy," especially at lunchtime, to "accept" students removed from class.

Forge on. Take courage. If, at meetings, neither you nor others have challenged the administrators on this misguided policy, be directed by, what seems to me, a simple rule of thumb. By words or actions or even attitude, if anyone has impeded learning within the classroom, has been offensive, that student will be removed. Stick to your guns. You are right. Let's hope that "the powers that be" catch on. Realize that you are actually helping both the offending student by establishing the structure of what will and will not be allowed, as well as the other students in your room.

Yelling is beneath you, as an educator and as a person. Used in large group settings, as previously mentioned (the cafeteria, the gym, the football field, for example) it is necessary just to be heard, perhaps. In a class? No.

17. ALSO, YOU ARE NOT MOTHER THERESA, RICKI LAKE, THEIR PARENT, OR THEIR FRIEND

Remember what your job is, what your goals for the students, for the classes are. Students understand fairness. A failing grade will not, on the whole, have a student hating you—once he calms down. He usually realizes and regrets his own "lacks," his poor attendance record, his lack of homework, his lack of studying, and his lack of seeking your assistance or of refusing your help. His anger, more than likely, is aimed at himself. Therefore, take heart. I've had teachers convey that they couldn't fail students because this one was so nice, or this one had family problems. Another was in a difficult relationship or going through a rough time. Some teachers have stated that they couldn't bear for their students not to like them.

Stop and think. Yes, firm and fair. And, yes, each student should be treated as an individual. And, no, getting too many breaks teaches most students that they'll always be cut some slack. And they have parents, the overwhelming number of whom are decent, caring, and devoted to their children's well being. **You** are not their friend. You are, most certainly, not their parent. You cannot be their rescuer either.

You can gather those in positions to help the youngsters; you can be supportive.

You must remember that you already have a very important role; you are their teacher, the one who will help make them more proficient in your subject, the one who will help them make genuine progress. You should be someone they respect and trust—not just because you are a decent human being. You are the teacher who works hard at her job—is intelligent, efficient, imaginative, and understanding. You are a professional educator.

We all want to be liked; but, for a teacher, that "like" should actually be respect. Some teachers spend a large amount of class time talking about their and their students' relationships, girlfriends and boyfriends, husbands and wives. Too much intimacy, too much sharing crosses the line, I believe; this is not Ricki Lake Nation. The scholastic classroom, the English classroom, for example, is not the venue for the cheap exploitation of teen problems or the vernacular that accompanies some TV shows. Be uplifting. You are the person who speaks well, articulates interestingly, uses no slang or jargon –and expects the best from the students, as well. Your classroom is not a TV show; it is not the street. It is a safe haven, a place of scholarship and respect. Most of your pupils will know this in short time.

18. SPEAK UP AT FACULTY MEETINGS

Not too frequently the first year, perhaps, but soon, very soon, give your reaction to the ideas expressed in meetings. Set forth some fresh ideas of your own, as well. Administrators are sometimes lulled into thinking that all is well, when it clearly is not, because some members of the faculty choose not to speak and have the limelight fall on them. Some veteran teachers may be apathetic; others just want the meeting over, having been "on stage," so to speak, for over five hours. There are educators who are simply afraid that the principal won't like them, while a few have learned that much is said, but little changes; therefore they have chosen not to join in the futility. Some of these rationales are understandable; all are unacceptable.

You state your ideas and try to enlist others to voice their concerns also. Administrators, who forge on, unchallenged, may think that the lack of discussion denotes assent. They probably never realized that "you have not converted a man because you have silenced him." Teachers, all of us, must speak out, especially about the things that are wrong—again and again, if necessary.

For example, if the lack of the administrators' support for teachers with students who are continually disruptive is demoralizing one or more teachers, say it out loud. Why you? Because it's right. There are always those who find it difficult, if not impossible, to defend themselves, to speak up for themselves. Help them. If necessary, speak for them.

Don't join the whining in the teachers' room, but do air

your concerns, your complaints, and your praise, as well. Be, as you are in the classroom: honest, intelligent, and respectful. That so many educators through the years have allowed themselves and others to be intimidated is a shame.

Mr. Language (during a meeting): "Is it true that Joe Jones was once again making noises and fresh remarks while Ms. Grammar was teaching? I bring this up to help you realize that there are many of us who are very frustrated that this goes on and on. He does the same thing in several of his classes, gets detention—or not—and "the beat goes on."

Mrs. Leader: "Now is not the place to discuss this."

Mr. G: "I respectfully disagree. It is not this particular student we wish to discuss at all, but the entire way such situations are handled. Can't you see that things keep getting worse? This boy and so many others receive little or no punishment; and you wait until he has misbehaved several times before you act, before you call his parents, and before you make his teachers aware that this is a continual and serious problem."

Mr. Leader: "I know how you feel. We've talked to the boy many times. What would you suggest we do?"

Ms. Social Studies: "You don't get it. We're not just speaking of this one student. We'd like to address the escalating misbehavior that we feel is the direct result of your desultory actions and/ or your inaction in too many instances." "There is strength in numbers."

No one likes to be challenged or contradicted, and certainly not in front of others. Principals are no different. Administrators, in spite of the fact that they all say, "My door is always open," have, in recent years, dealt with many student behaviors in a clandestine fashion. Therefore, their "door" is not always open. They do not want you shedding light sometimes on conduct they wish to keep out of the general knowledge of the teachers or the school committee or the community. How ironic that they feel the same thing that they impose on their teachers: that to admit problems, that to act on some problems openly would, in fact, have them appear as weak and incompetent.

You are entitled to bring up issues that affect the classroom, that relate to morale, etc.; in fact, you must. Things will be solved far more readily if you bring attention to them. Now that seems logical, doesn't it? So do it. Take heart. Give the administrators the opportunity to keep the faculty informed of their progress and to alleviate these bad situations.

You will gain the respect of your colleagues, the administrators and, most importantly, you will be cognizant of the fact that you did the right thing. It will not affect you adversely, for your bosses will realize that you are someone to be reckoned with. Remember, as well, that you will be helping those misbehaving students.

19. USE JOURNALS (ENGLISH CLASSES) NOT AS DIARIES, BUT AS A PLACE FOR THEM TO PRACTICE WHAT THEY LEARN AND TO EXPERIMENT WITH STYLES, GENRES, AND CONSTRUCTION. THEY CAN ALSO SERVE AS AN EMOTIONAL OUTLET.

Journals can become very time-consuming for the teacher, for they should be checked periodically with comments jotted in the pages to the writer. "Most interesting turn of phrase about your love of soccer. Keep up your original work. I enjoyed noting your progress, Nick." Or "Please don't scribble, for it's too hard to read." Or "I got the general idea and suggest that our discussion of using lively verbs might come into play here. Try some and return this to me please. I'm eager to see the rewrite, Sue."

I loved using journals, and they enjoyed writing in their journals. I just couldn't keep up with checking them. Remember we're speaking of over 100 journals with multiple entries. Therefore, try to check them, at least, every month.

The lesson is done, and the homework needs to be completed elsewhere? Say, "Take out your journals for the last twenty minutes. For you who cannot come up with your own topic, I'll put a couple of suggestions on the board. Let's begin."

The "rules" for journals: explain exactly why you use them and encourage them as writers:

- No inappropriate language: swearing and vulgarities are not acceptable. Some of the Jerry Springer School of Educators regard journals as the students' personal diaries and think that telling them that there will be no "correct" or "incorrect," regarding the journal writing makes the student like the teacher. Young, inexperienced teachers feel that allowing them free reign makes the youngsters feel important and makes their relationship with the student more on an equal basis. Balderdash! (I love that old-fashioned epithet.) School is never the place to be insolent or crude. They cannot fall back on swearing. Most who claim they must use that kind of language to be realistic simply never tried another way. Teach them.

- Let them know that writing can be an adventure. Tell them to date each entry. You and they can become aware, thereby, of improved phrasing, of the variety of topics, of the use of figures of speech, etc. Instruct them to use the journals whenever they feel like writing, as well as when the teacher assigns an entry. They are theirs to discuss ideas, to construct a poem about life, to begin an essay on injustice, or to detail the conversation from the previous night at the family dinner table.

- When they get the hang of all this, they think it's fun. And it is. The teacher should be ready with some topics, for "I can't think of anything to write about" is not acceptable. The journal is a regular and unconstrained place to practice writing. "How can it be termed "uncon-

73

strained," if you won't let us write what we want?" Ah, swearing and obscenities is what you want to write? No, it is beneath us to do this; and, quite frankly, I do not want to read those kinds of things. I am asking you to find a better way to say what you have to say.

- "You do not have to check your entry for grammar or spelling, so that you will be encouraged to deal with both ideas and style—to write and write and write and write. You will choose one entry a month to edit, to rewrite for me, your favorite entry, perhaps the one you think is written the best or is most interesting. This will hone your skill in the edit process, too. You will go back and put a check on any entry you find too personal to share with me, and I will not read those. May I assure you that what you write, however, is between you and me. I will not reveal what you have written, unless I feel that you or another is in danger, in need of help."

- Sometimes give twenty to thirty minutes to do an entry right in class; sometimes make that the homework assignment. If students are done with much of the assigned work, make it a class routine that journals can then be used.

They will gradually delight in their own expression and their own improvement and take pride in their entries. Your brief comments, your feedback becomes important to them; and they look forward to reading your reactions.

20. DO NOT IGNORE BAD BEHAVIOR OR LANGUAGE IN THEIR ACTIONS, THEIR SPEECH— OR THEIR WRITING

So much of the bounds you set may seem repetitive, but the structure becomes important for the students. They should clearly know what is condoned in your classroom. One difficulty is that some teachers allow—or ignore—actions and/or language that you do not. "Gee, what's the big deal? So, I said, 'Pissa.' So what? Miss Botany and Mr. Art don't mind. I say it in their classes all the time."

"Here, we aim for better language. You're a smart person, and you already know that your language is not, in here, the language of the streets or what may be deemed acceptable in other places. Here, I expect you to be my scholars. I expect the words you use to be ones of respect, of intelligence. Think about it. What is the sense of learning the beautiful turn of phrase, the figurative language, and the good grammar if not to make them yours—for life? So, we may say that we practice that concept every day. And, I might add, you know that already; it just takes a bit of reminding you from time to time."

A new teacher, who actually had some private school experience, kept teetering back and forth between two modes of action. She would press on with the lesson and ignore the foul language punctuating the air, being aimed at one student then another. She also would pretend not to see students get out of their seats at will, while she was at the board, discussing the homework. A boy walked down the aisle, threw something in the basket, walked up another aisle, and punched his friend in the arm. He then walked down that aisle and returned to his seat, smugly grinning.

She just forged on, rattling off answers, calling on students, and never acknowledging the remarks that were rife in her classroom every day or the students who chose to stroll whenever they pleased. A perfect example of a teacher who, though aggressive by nature, had been intimidated and refused to admit that fact. The uncooperative youngsters in her room had been allowed to misbehave too long. Then when her private conversations with them, her calls to a parent, and her personal approach simply kept failing, time after time, she finally sent them to the office. There, they would occasionally receive detention; most of the time they never went. They took a stroll around the building or went to the boys' room and hung out.

When they did report to the office, there they were privy to another heart-to-heart, this time from the Assistant Principal, who then would state, "He's not a bad boy." So what? And who said he was? This capricious attention obviously cured nothing; and the misbehavior, of course, continued.

Not wanting to admit that problems still arose daily in her classes, she dealt with them by not dealing with them. "Oh, yes, everything is much better now. I'm just too busy to discuss anything right now; and, besides, everything is fine." Sure.

Support and consistency were needed. The problems, the poor behavior persisted. Some students learned in spite of the atmosphere. Some were denied that opportunity because the school and/or the teacher didn't make them be students. To choose the easy way is really such a cop-out; for, in reality, it isn't easy. To tolerate insolence, insubordination, or foul language tacitly or openly isn't easy for a teacher to do. This young woman had the potential to be a fine teacher. She was exuberant, intelligent, and dedicated. The pupils' "excuses" are that they're immature; they're children. What are the excuses of the teacher, the administrators, and the school?

You allow it, and it doesn't just go away. You allow it; and, by the time the warm weather comes, you'll be an insomniac; and they'll be worse. You allow it, and you'll be taking Tylenol PM every night. At the end of the next year, she left.

For too many classes, public school just isn't private school; at least, that's what the teacher thought she learned, that they just couldn't be well behaved. Too bad. There should be no difference in the atmosphere or the behavior of the youngsters in private or public school.

21. VARY LESSONS AND PROCEDURES FROM TIME TO TIME

Every Friday certainly can be vocabulary day, if you so choose; but every once in a while shake it up. Have a journal-writing day. Connect to a discussion that came up that week. Toss out an association to the present from the reading, say, of Poe or *Macbeth*. Announce that you are breaking from the routine and query whether they have an issue to discuss (that relates to the course), or is there a skill they feel that needs a bit of extra explanation or review. It breathes a bit of fresh air to do this once in a while.

"We usually review the homework today (or we usually do the next vocabulary lesson, etc.), but today let's continue with *Macbeth* because your oral presentations yesterday were quite wonderful. I so enjoyed the obvious comprehension of the characters' motivations that you showed; and I delighted in your acting talents, as well, that I would like you to entertain me again today. We'll take up the vocabulary next week."

Today, let's put our desks in a circle and read aloud to one another that portion of your paper that you feel represents your best writing. Let's share our paragraphs that we've worked hard on, that incorporate those things we've learned about imagery, interesting verbs, onomatopoeia, etc. Let's show off to each other and give and get support. "David, you begin with that exciting story of your job in the bank, please."

"The quarter has ended, and today we begin anew. Let's all have different seats. C'mon, now. All those at the back will be nearer the front—the expensive seats. Those on the right side will be in the middle or the left side. You left-siders will move to the center or the right. Not such a big change, but a new perspective." Look over the new arrangement, which takes about two minutes to accomplish; and check that girls and boys are mixed; that friends who chat are separated; that they are, in fact, surrounded by new faces. Now make a final check that all can see and hear well, and that "bad actors" are surrounded by those who would never allow others to be a class distraction. Fresh start.

22. DRESS APPROPRIATELY

Most teachers use common sense and good taste in their attire. It is important for you to be the teacher, dressed in clothing that is clean and comfortable; yet, though you are not compelled to don a business suit each day, a teacher should dress in a manner that conveys that you are not the youngsters' peer. You are neither a camp counselor, nor a ragamuffin. Some teachers wear unpressed shirts that look like they've slept in them. The lumberjack and dungaree ensemble does not belong in the classroom. Shorts or sneakers are not suitable for teachers. Yes, very casual clothing should be worn searching in the woods with your charges or for let's-clean-the-whole-room period or today-we-paint day, etc. There has to be a common-sensical element to your work clothes.

Your attire should be that of an adult, a professional, an educator. If you cannot wear shoes, find something that is more acceptable than sneakers. Actually, today there are so many styles to choose from, it would be so easy to find sneaker substitutes that lend more of a professional appearance.

Students, too, should dress appropriately, following a dress code that students, faculty, and administrators have approved. Who wears hats indoors? Not acceptable. Short shorts or bare midriffs? Not acceptable. This is a place to teach youngsters not to cave in to fads.

23. CREATE BULLETIN BOARDS THAT REINFORCE THE LESSONS, DISPLAY THE STUDENTS' WORK, AND THAT INSPIRE.

Put up the best of their writing, the poems, the essays, as well as the tests. Hang up those that show improvement, too. Tell the classes about each one. Encourage them to check the boards frequently because every couple of weeks or so you will change the items and proudly hang a new display of their fine work on tests, projects, illustrations, poems, and essays, etc. Display their extra credit work, too.

You're studying figures of speech, so display the terms and examples. You've been discussing propaganda techniques; put up their original ads and some professional ones. You've been reading war poetry, put up some famous poems and some war photos, perhaps, along with some student samples.

Put up pithy quotes that are funny or famous and/or inspire, so that your students are constantly surrounded by learning, by background information:

- "Never let the fear of striking out get in your way."— Babe Ruth
- "Neither a borrower or a lender be."—William Shakespeare
- "I had a lover's quarrel with the world."—Robert Frost
- "Fame is a bee,
  It has a song,
  It has a sting,
  Ah, too, it has a wing."—Emily Dickinson

24. UTILIZE THE LIBRARY—AND THE LIBRARIAN

Librarians today are "media specialists." They are the jacks-of-all-trades, being knowledgeable about sound systems and video cameras, VCR's and projectors, copy machines and fax machines, computers and the Internet, printers and DVD's. There is less emphasis on using books for research and more on gathering sources on the Net, and the librarians are very skilled at this.

Discuss with your librarian the ways which she can assist you and your classes. For example, the librarian gives your groups "a tour" through the many resources that are available to the students and how to access them efficiently. You and the librarian can jointly plan a research unit, and the librarian can assist you in choosing videos to incorporate into a unit of study. She has much to offer, being so multi-talented; so avail yourself of her experience.

25. BEGIN EACH MARKING PERIOD AND EACH YEAR WITH A CLEAN SLATE.

James Russell Lowell must have had school in mind, as well as life in general, when he proclaimed, "Each day the world is born anew." Every marking period, every year, students have the opportunity to begin again. Give them that chance. Would that life was as generous as school, giving that *tabula rasa* to us every quarter of a year.

Clear away the old notions, the cobwebs, and tell them to do the same. New year, new dedication. I always thought that students were so fortunate to get a new try each term and not be impeded by their performance of the previous quarter. Tell them. Remind them that this does not mirror life. For all my theories that school is a microcosm of life, this is not one of those times, thank goodness. Some school policies, devised years ago, give our young people every opportunity. Caught up in the whirl of technology and testing, we forget that at its inception, educational institutions created procedures to give each child every chance to learn and succeed. One of these is the dividing of the school year into terms, even if the student is taking the same course. New quarter, new commitment. It's like a breath of ocean air, fresh and clean.

26. AFFORD THEM MANY OPPORTUNITIES TO SHOW PROGRESS

In order to be fair, when giving the term grade or the final grade, a teacher should have many marks and a variety of skills tested to use for the assessment. A few teachers may get caught up in, heaven knows what, falling in love with their own voices, perhaps, and neglect the quizzes, the tests, the papers, or the homework. How can you judge a student's progress, his commitment to studying with only five or six-or less-grades?

Test regularly. Give them credit for their homework, their class participation, and their extra credit work. Assign a hierarchy of skills (opening paragraphs, the body or research of a paper, outlines, thesis statements, concluding paragraphs, first drafts, final drafts). And give them the credit they earn, so they can have a barometer reading as to how they are faring each step of the way. Give practices tests and help them from one stage to the next. Let them learn that it's "as ye sow, so shall ye reap." Think of it as the grand harvest that has been taking place all term, and now all the grades are gathered in.

26. ASSIGN HOMEWORK REGULARLY: TO REINFORCE THE LESSON; TO GIVE TIME TO DO RESEARCH; TO HAVE THEM HAVE QUIET TIME TO STUDY, TO READ, TO WRITE, TO AID COMPREHENSION; TO DRILL; TO USE THEIR IMAGINATIONS.

I do not agree with the current homework theories for elementary grade children. Newspapers are always filled with how our students do not fare as well as those in other countries. Always. So, not too many years ago, some great minds in education decided that all children needed to have nightly homework, even the very young. They mollified those that looked askance at this policy by stating that the assignment(s) would be small ones and recommending that parents get involved with each night's home lessons.

What pressure on youngsters (not to mention parents). "Oh, no, they love it." "My husband and I enjoy helping little Timmy. Every night, right after dinner, he goes over his vocabulary lesson and his arithmetic work with us before he goes to bed." I hear this about such small children.

And the assignments grew longer and more complex with time, and the pressure was on. Let's not make a third grader have that daily strain with the additional stress of mom and dad "helping." That's not what we want. "Well, we'll certainly beat those kids from Japan," is what we hear.

Let them play outside and, perhaps, have one school task to perform, i.e. read a short story or poem; draw a home scene (this is supper time at our house); do an arithmetic problem; find a picture in a magazine of, say, a mixture of vivid colors. Have them write in their notebook what task they performed, so they can tell or show the teacher and classmates. More than this, yes, yes, they could handle. But should they?

They're children—in need of fresh air and playing after school with their friends and their pets and just sitting and imagining or coloring in their coloring books or digging in the yard.

Mom and dad are mom and dad, not the teachers. Mom and dad work hard at jobs and cleaning and shopping and cooking and so many other things during the day. Parents could, of course, answer a question or give a BIT of assistance and continue to read a story to or with them, of course—but that's all. That's enough.

I've witnessed parents who write whole papers or type entire papers or drill their children over and over again. Some have created project models worthy of being marketed for their children's assignments. There have been many cases of those in supervisory positions at their own work who have had their fellow workers or their own employees do research; build; write, edit; and/or type their offsprings' assignments. And proud of it. What wonderful object lessons for the children.

Students, as do we all, learn by doing (or not doing). We learn from not only success; we learn from mistakes. Let them learn; and let their work be just that, their work.

Starting, perhaps, in the 5th or 6th grade, the homework

could be of a bit more substantial nature and complexity. A bit. And by the time they are in junior high, they can begin to have "real homework." The homework policy should be discussed among the faculty, and the procedures set should be agreed upon and carried out. The fact that some teachers give much too much, and some teachers give no homework at all should give everyone pause. Parents should be involved in checking on this particular aspect, namely how often is homework assigned, as well as the quality and amount.

Just because the assignment takes Dan a great deal of time does not indicate that the work is too difficult or the assignment too long. Common sense has to rear its head. Some students neglect daily assignments, so that finally it takes much time to complete the work, due to their own prior disregard. They play catch up, so to speak.

If a junior or senior gets home at three o'clock, has a snack, takes a breath, and begins the work, he can, perhaps, get in two hours before dinner. Another two or three hours should do it, giving enough time to study four or five hours a day. For high school students, this should be sufficient time to accomplish the assignments, organize thoughts, and prepare for the next day. Enough!

And when are we going to tackle the difficult discussion of the large number of students who work after school and on weekends? Or those who engage in sports? Or extra curricular activities? Do we really believe that these students can possibly complete four or five quality hours of homework? Most don't even do two!

27. BE GENEROUS WITH ENCOURAGEMENT AND PRAISE, BOTH ORAL AND WRITTEN, RECOGNIZING IMPROVEMENT, ORIGINALITY, EFFORT, AND EXCELLENCE

Say your praise out loud. Say it clearly to the student and to the class—about a response, a test, a journal entry, or re-

83

port. Commend an answer or a piece of extra credit. Sprinkle your compliments liberally; so your students know that you are aware of their efforts, their attempts, and their study.

"Donald, what a moving tribute you wrote; we'll have to publish that."

"Class, your project work so impressed me that I want to take a moment at the beginning of the period to stop and give you the applause you deserve. You will notice that all your papers are on display on the boards, and I want you to get up and take a look at the burst of creativity that made me so proud of all of you."

"Keep up the fine work, Karen; your phrasing moved me."

"Now you've got it. Fine job, Caroline."

28. BRING IN THE WORLD

Connect the work, when possible, to events in the news, as well as to positive values. Deal with the motivations of the classic characters in their readings and those on the world stage today. Use videos, art, music, software, TV, and drama—everything that can make a lesson come to life and/or add a touch of imagination and interest. This takes organization and planning. What you are doing by making these connections and adding the texture of the arts is reinforcing the lessons, the assignments, and the class discussions.

President Bush's statement would illustrate the very lessons that the class had been discussing. "We will not tire; we will not falter, and we will not fail." What a fine example of repetition, of rhythm, and of alliteration.

Years ago, there was a bill that would have allowed young people doing the same work as older workers to be paid less due to their age. It was deemed an "incentive" and called a "differential" and labeled an "opportunity." What it would have done was permit employers of the young people in the country to pay the thousands of kids less for, say, flipping burgers than the adults standing next to them, also flipping burgers. It was a grand way to discuss *1984* and the use of euphemisms. An "incentive," indeed! And the "differential" was the difference between a fair wage and a con job. Those sponsoring the bill tried to convince their colleagues that for teens to have a chance at a job at all was an "opportunity." The students understood the power of the wording all too well; and, once again, the brilliance of Orwell shone.

As "Auntie Mame" said, "Life's a banquet." Help your pupils enjoy the feast. Bring in videos; do experiments; play music; take them to the movies. Immerse them in the joy of learning. After all, isn't that why you chose to teach? Didn't you think that learning was a joy?

When we were doing *Romeo and Juliet* and *Macbeth*, I brought to school dozens of crowns and baubles and scarves and beads. I festooned myself with necklaces and a bejeweled tiara, as we did the readings; and gradually they arose, helped themselves to a crown or necklace, and got into the spirit. Plastic glasses filled with grape juice also put us in the mood for the Shakespearean parties; and we toasted our author and his famous creations—and ourselves, of course.

We, the students and I, brought in songs that told a story and songs that had our figures of speech. It was so entertaining to play them for the classes, as we discussed why we chose this particular lyric or what the melody conveyed. We sang them, and some students chose to write original songs and perform them for us. It was thrilling—and it made our study of the use of language, our figures of speech, or our unit in poetry special.

Students have overwhelmed me with their creative outbursts:

—A talented, young lady wrote poetry about Macbeth and Lady Macbeth and illustrated her own work in brilliantly colored oils and put it all on a window shade that could be pulled down to display to the classes.

—Student/musicians created folk songs, based on the short

85

stories we read and strummed and strolled around the class, serenading us..

—One bright and fun-loving boy built a maze and brought both cheese and a real mouse for his project on *Flowers for Algernon*. We gazed in awe, as his "Algernon" ran the well-constructed maze, seeking his reward. We had such fun, appreciating his original idea. (Had the mouse not bitten the poor youngster, prompting us to have the nurse take our imaginative student to the hospital, we would have still been enjoying the creativity.)

—We were treated to a symphony written by a student as a memorial to the victims of the Holocaust, after reading books and stories and poems about the tragedy.

—An ethnic feast, along with the recipes and the background of the dishes was our "gift" from some clever student chefs, upon finishing stories and discussions of those with varied backgrounds.

—Students wrote wonderful love poems and stories, complicated and moving, when we finished our poetry unit. Shakespeare and Edna St. Vincent Millay had nothing on them.

—We were the audience for home videos on Shakespeare and a video that utilized "man-in-the-street" interviews, dealing with the plight of the homeless.

—One young man, who I am certain is now in Hollywood plying his craft, wrote a long and involved, full length movie script for us.

I could go on forever with the outpouring of talent, of learning, of genuine pleasure.

I have sat in on classes taught by Ms. Social Studies or Mr. Math and been so engaged, so inspired with the discussions, the use of the newspaper, the stock market, and tales of Julius Caesar in the latter, and the use of primary source material, of videos of Nazi Germany, of intelligent discourse on the backgrounds of historical figures in the former, to mention just a few examples of these "master classes"—and "master teachers."

The creativity in Ms. Art's classes reinforced the idea that teachers have to communicate with other teachers, visit other classrooms. The wondrous outpouring of beautiful, expressive, and original paintings and drawings and sculptures astounded me. Some of my charges who were not good English students, for example, were, in fact, marvelous artists.

29. DON'T TAKE FOR GRANTED WHAT THEY KNOW OR THEIR PERSONAL LIVES

Surprise is omnipresent in teaching. How they take to certain writers, how fast they assimilate a unit's objective varies within classes and individual students. Many people assume that students all have common knowledge, basic teachings. Nay, not so.

A colleague recounted that he found, during a discussion in his English class, that several of his eighth graders couldn't tell time. They were amazed that 11:45 and quarter of 12 were, in fact, the same time. He soon proceeded to build in a lesson on reading the clock. He was experienced and knew that the correct thing to do was "to give them what they didn't have." He was alert and experienced—another example of good teaching, as he wove this into his English lesson.

Once, having to substitute for an absent social studies teacher who had left a series of maps for his class, I learned a lesson. The class was coloring away, copying from the text and using the information in the geography book to learn about the countries assigned. A sweet, little girl called out rather wistfully that she'd love to visit the country she was learning about. I asked her why she had chosen that particular country; and her response was, "I want to see a place where the ground is so pink." So the lesson then had to include a discussion on the nature of maps.

During summer school one year, I handed out rulers to the class for their project work. The stack of rulers was a conglomeration of all the rulers I had collected through my many years. Some were thin, wooden ones; some were also of wood, but larger and heavier. Others were of brightly-colored plastic, red, green, light blue, white, and yellow. Within my circus of measures were the more "modern" ones, as well. These lightweight rulers were also brightly colored in neon hues and translucent to boot, bright orange and cotton-candy pink and lemon yellow. They were passed up and down the aisles with each vying for his favorite instrument. Then I heard a rumbling, as some were voicing their displeasure at receiving a certain color. "What, what, what? What is the matter?"

"My ruler measures different than Christina's."

"Yeah, it's not fair." Kevin's is different than mine."

"Different how?" I asked. They're all the same, as far as measuring goes. They are just rulers in various colors."

"What? But hers is bigger (or wider or heavier or brighter or has larger numbers or has darker print)."

"I repeat they are all the same. They each measure twelve inches, one foot."

"No, that can't be. Do you mean to tell us that all these school rulers measure the same?"

"That's exactly what I am telling you."

"Wow. We didn't know that."

"Ms. Tanner, when is the word "I" capitalized?"

"The word "I" –meaning yourself—is always capital-ized."

"Even when it's not at the beginning of a sentence?" continues this junior.

"Yes, it is always a capital letter."

"I never knew that!"

AS students begin to know you and start to trust you, they will share their dreams, their fears, their joys, their past, not just with you, but with the class, as well. In turn, the classes are "trained" to be attentive, constructive in their comments, and supportive. "That was so terrific, Jeff; boy, are you brave." The boys and girls begin to feel at ease and comfortable, and a we're-all-in-this-together bond is created.

The rule was that no one had to share writing he deemed too personal with the class and that I would keep private all but the things I thought put them or others in danger. Gradually, many wanted to share, however, telling of a struggle with bulimia, feelings of rejection by a friend, the day parents gave away a family dog "without telling." Some would relate the happiness of a first crush, or how they just loved to play their sports, or the feelings conjured up due to a parent's alcoholism. I read glorious tales of the warmth and pleasure of the family barbecue and of the day it dawned that the girl next door became the love of one's life.

Teenage adventures were rife in our creative writing sessions, like the time the locals were chased by a group from the next town, and fists went flying, all because these boys were out-of-towners. This piece was one of wit and humor and was also profound. The candor, the freshness of expression, the genuine talent that continually surfaced delighted us all. I felt it was a privilege that we could relate our feelings—not only unafraid, but so well.

There are days that teachers question why they still do this job. Then again, there are many days, like these, listening to these intimacies, that moved me, writings that were so cogent, so articulate that I used to feel I should pay the town for my having such a good time. **Getting paid to do a job you love and are good at is, arguably, the greatest gift in life.**

30. JOIN WITH COLLEAGUES FOR A CORE APPROACH WHEN POSSIBLE

There are units of study that lend themselves to a core approach, seeking to lessen the fragmentation of study. The goal is for the students to have an overview, a more complete picture of an era, a writer, etc. This requires time for the teachers to sit and plan and coordinate; usually, this kind of time is never built in to a schedule. The teachers devise a plan to work together and fit the logistics in themselves, working after school or at their homes and often at night or on weekends.

A study of the Holocaust, using textbooks, primary source material, and videos was presented. We included writings of those directly involved, as well as material from "Facing History and Ourselves." This was organized jointly working with a fine history teacher, the same Ms. Social Studies referred to earlier, and the additional help of the art teacher, the librarian, and the music director.

It turned out to be an amazing unit, filled with the historical background, as well as the severity, the angst, the cruelty, the apathy—so many emotions. It elicited such creativity on the part of the students. They wrote music; they filled essays with research and understanding and outrage. They spun poetry and created plays that would make one weep. Their artistic visions captured this aberration so well. Not only did they dazzle us with their talent, they learned well the historical data and the propaganda techniques.

It was a study that was rigorous and creative—and cooperative.

The "experts" have ever recommended the core approach (as if the experienced teacher was oblivious of its value!); but, evidently, they never told administrators how to allot planning time or how to coordinate the various schedules to accomplish it. When it can be done, do it. It is actually such an organized and thrilling experience for the students—and the teachers also.

31. MAKE YOUR STUDENTS ACTIVE, RATHER THAN PASSIVE, LEARNERS—EVEN ON LESSONS THAT STRESS LISTENING SKILLS, VIDEOS, OR ORAL PRESENTATIONS.

Planning and organizing are very important, as I'm sure you've noticed by now. You need to know where the lesson, the unit is going, meaning what you will include to afford many opportunities for them to demonstrate their new learning, what materials and methods will broaden the interest, and how they can be active participants.

When the plan includes a video clip, a piece of music, or a movie, have a question sheet prepared and discuss it *before* the viewing. That way they will be able to look for certain facts or symbolism or acting nuances or dialogue, etc., while watching. If you just turn on "the show," too many of them sit back and relax, shall we say, a bit too much. Have the question sheet filled out upon completion of the film or tape and collect it and mark it, and/or discuss it. Do something, so they will learn how to be involved listeners and viewers.

The same is true when the class is presenting individual projects or papers. Prepare a peer-evaluation grading sheet and teach the class about constructive criticism and what is meant by "helpful suggestions." Put the categories on the board and discuss the fact that the combination of all these elements comprises a good editorial, for example. Leave a place for helpful suggestions and have the class fill in the sheet after each speaker, reminding them that it is not a speech class, but the inability to hear a speaker certainly might be considered in the evaluation, under the item, "delivery," perhaps. Teach them to focus on what you have taught them about the essay.

For example,

- Is it clear to the readers/audience what the topic is?
- Is the writer's position on the topic clear?
- Was time and effort expended on turn of phrase?
- Is the title/headline "a grabber?"
- Does the body contain facts to support the writer's position?
- Are there quotations included from credible sources?
- Does the writer acknowledge any opposing view?
- Is the vocabulary engaging?
- Were any literary techniques in evidence, i.e. imagery, alliteration, similes, metaphors, etc.?
- Does the conclusion restate the position in some way and tie up the ends, so to speak?
- Was the paper interesting?
- How was the delivery—voice (clear, loud enough, slow enough, good enunciation)?
- Was there any eye contact with audience?
- Emotions (sincere, where necessary—smiling, where needed)
- Did the speaker pause when needed?
- How was the posture? Did the writer stand and not slouch over the podium, not weave back and forth, not keep his hands in his pockets, not chew gum?

Some or all these could be among the comments on the evaluation sheet, which can be scanned briefly by the teacher before collecting and distributing to each individual writer. The students then stay on their toes and involved, rather than sitting there, passively, blankly, or apathetically.

32. ENCOURAGE CREATIVITY, ORIGINALITY, DRAMATIC PRESENATIONS—EXPERIMENTATIONS

Encourage their creative inventions. Suggest ways to enhance a written project with a skit or a one-act play, perhaps. Some of these students haven't had an outlet for artistic expression within a scholastic discipline in a long time, so you be the patron. They could do a painting, a collage of magazine illustrations, a comic strip, a movie poster, or a set of photographs. You will be able to encourage them to try out genres from a prior unit, i.e. to write an epic poem or a TV sitcom to be performed in the classroom. Help them envision their perception by their making a video of *Macbeth* with class members in the roles. They could try their hand at writing a soliloquy or the music and/or lyrics to a song about their topic.

Fill the class with enthusiasm for experimentation.

Display their projects all over the room. Set aside "performance days," which will delight the class (and thrill you). Praise their creations and play a part, as well.

You join in and offer your own work, "putting your money where your mouth is," so to speak. I've written—and performed—my original—and not yet famous—song, "I Am 'Johnny Tremain.'" I've done essays, odes, and plays. I've even painted my concept of scenes from famous novels and plays. Original pieces were performed by my students and by me; and, I must admit, I had such fun entertaining them and being entertained. Sharing my editorial columns was both an outlet for me and a source (I hope) of inspiration for them.

93

33. STATE THE PURPOSE OF THE CLASS, THE DAY'S LESSON OR UNIT, AND OFFER A RECAPITULATION AT THE CLOSE OF THE PERIOD AND/OR THE END OF THE UNIT. "WHAT DID WE LEARN?"

It lends structure and organization, as well as understanding, for students to know why they are doing what they are doing. "We are holding a grammar review because I want to pause right here and right now to ensure that, before you leave this year, you can turn all those years of studying grammar rules into empowerment. We will review the rules, so you can write an essay or a business letter or an application with no grammatical errors. The reason is that your readers should be able to concentrate on your ideas and that those ideas should be clear; your use of good grammar and punctuation will enable them to do that."

The students may be older now, more mature, and more able to recognize the necessity of knowing how to write with clarity; therefore, a brief review may, at this time, be more meaningful to them. You must also be aware that some teachers never drill in grammar or neglect to make its study part of the writing experience at all, and/or never or rarely hold students accountable for grammar proficiency. It is up to you, especially if you notice a deficiency in their skills, to hold such a review and to tell them why in a positive way.

"Now what did we learn today?"

"I learned that it's not so tough to share your writing," said the heretofore reticent journalism student.

"I learned that it is very important to give facts to back up your position."

"I learned all those comma uses, and they're not so hard."

34. DON'T LIE TO YOUR STUDENTS

Being candid with your students is a must. You cannot allow yourself to be trapped into euphemistic/hyperbolic evasions. These youngsters should be able to trust your words, to trust you.

Administrator: "Although 60% of 10th graders failed the test, we're encouraged by the 1% improvement rate over last year," stated an administrative press release. Even local newspapers hailed the improvement. That the media and the school spokespeople "loaded" their reporting of scores with this "feel good" palaver was an object lesson for students of writing. More than half a class fails a test and administrators and others contend it's their job to turn that into something positive? Something is wrong here.

To analyze the scores, to ascertain what parts of the frameworks, of the schools' curricula were deficient—that was their job. To monitor more closely their teachers to ensure that all were teaching the designated units and teaching well, testing regularly, assigning homework regularly, helping students, etc.—that was the administration's job. It also was their role to tell the public just that. To obfuscate the issue of low scores by circumlocution, however, became their mission.

35. REMEMBER HOW GOOD IT FEELS TO BE TREATED WITH COURTESY. TREAT YOUR STUDENTS IN THE SAME FASHION.

Most teachers treat their charges politely and fairly. Some, however, bark out orders in a brusque fashion and behave as if they're the old-time coaches, speaking in a harsh "I'll-show-them-who's-the-boss manner. There also are teachers who cross the line, who treat their students as their buddies, their pals. What these "chums" soon learn (and some never do) is that they do not get the best work out of their students, who evidently decide that they can slack off with their good buddy in charge.

Respect—remembering that you are their teacher, the purveyor of knowledge—and courtesy must be your guide. "Please" and "thank you" are for everyone, not just the students. It is up to you to set the tone of polite and respectful behavior and to expect to receive no less. "Thank you, Joe, for helping Felicia with her assignment. That was so nice of you."

36. SHOW YOUR PASSION, YOUR DELIGHT, AND YOUR ENTHUSIASM FOR THE SUBJECT YOU TEACH AND THE WORK YOUR STUDENTS DO.

You should verbalize that the lines in a poem move and delight you, that an article was "right on." You should discuss what emotions and reactions they conjure up.

I assigned Robert Frost's *Home Burial* for the class to read silently; I then read it aloud straight through. There's something sui generis about that particular poem, and I shared my ideas with them, after they gave me their interpretations. The words, the ideas seem so bone cold to me. Yet the imagery is magical here. Tell them. Tell them it thrills you to experience the power of such technique and feeling.

How magnificent an achievement to be able to cram so much into that poem, so much that is today, as well as yesterday, so much pain and both overt and subdued anger. What a genius was Frost to write in his many poems about nature and the land, and growing up and growing old, of love and beauty, and of prejudice, and tradition, of bravery and inspiration, of history and pride—and so much more. Tell them that. Tell them that it fills you with wonder and admiration. It "rocks your world."

Don't be stiff upper lip. Let loose. If you do, they will, too—gradually.

Kim: "That article in the *Boston Globe* made me so angry. Let me read those parts that infuriated me."

Jessie: "Ms. Tanner, we listen to those lyrics [rap lyrics] without caring what they say; it's not the way the columnist [Mike Barnicle, then of the *Boston Globe*] says about us. I laughed because he's so out of touch." (I agreed with the columnist; and a heavy discussion, so healthy, ensued.)

Amy: "Edna St. Vincent Millay really spoke to me in that poem about the man that treats his wife as his pet. 'What a big book for such a little head.' That's such a great line. I can understand why she is one of your favorite poets."

37. DON'T SPEAK IN CLICHES NOR ALLOW THEM TO DO SO.

Once students learn about clichés, they avoid them, for the most part, in their writing. Their speaking is another matter. It's no wonder, really, for they're surrounded by movies and TV with C-grade shows that are riddled with predictable situations and dialogue. For that matter, listen to the speeches at most graduations. Evan people in positions of authority evidently were ever too busy to come up with a fresh vision or expression. They spout, year after year after year, that education is a key, a door, a bridge, a path, a window. And education is each and every one of these and more, yet it is the task of the teacher to make it understandable that it behooves every speaker and writer to say what he has to say in an original way, to take a fresh approach.

Don't approve of those who glom onto the easy way, rather than do individual thinking. Thus, make Shaun try again when he says that he wants "to be all he can be." Commend the sentiments, noting that the Army came up with it as a catchy slogan, and assign him the task of saying the same thing in his own creative way.

Suggest to Alicia that she come up with an "Alicia expression" to describe her mother, other than "she has a heart of gold."

38. GIVE EXTRA CREDIT, AN ADDITIONAL ACKNOWLEDGEMENT, IF YOU WILL, TO THOSE WHO CONNECT THE CLASSWORK TO ANOTHER BOOK, A NEWS OR MAGAZINE ARTICLE, A PLAY, A TV SHOW.

It's actually fun to watch them realize that "the outside world" uses "their" vocabulary words, discusses some of the same topics they do in class. They bring in books for you to recognize they found the words, or a magazine article that deals with the conflicts in tradition, "just like we talked about yesterday." Put their name on the articles. Display them and call attention to them in class. Make everyone aware that Josh found the article in the *New York Times* and that he is getting a point in your rank book.

39. REMIND THEM, FROM TIME TO TIME, OF THE GOALS OF THE CLASS, THE RULES, AND THE STANDARDS

We all need reminders; and these are energetic, young people whose lives are crammed with so much. It is your job to remind them of the fact that, once we enter, we sit down, etc. They will occasionally forget and rush to respond to a classmate's opinion, for example. Refresh their memories as to the rules (and the reasons for them). Enthusiasm and involvement are welcome, but the boundaries are set to allow free expression, to encourage individual ideas, to be fair and polite always.

When students get engrossed in an extra curricula activity, such as Student Council or a sport or the musical, they often neglect their studies. Their advisors are zealots for their special project and look away when a rehearsal or a meeting or a practice keeps pumped up pupils at school until the wee hours. Their grades and attention plummet, for they're simply too exhausted to do the quality of work of which they are capable.

Students need to be reminded at such a juncture that their special event is, indeed, important; but their studies are more so. It is a shame that some of their sponsors, the adult supervisors, can't keep this in mind. Confide this to them.

40. DEAL WITH PARENTS WITH PATIENCE AND CANDOR

Most parents are wonderful to deal with. They are empathetic, supportive, and interested in your perspective. They open up to you and respect the work you do. I became friendly with many parents, understanding their involvement and concern. Many have made me cookies, helped out as chaperones on a field trip, written warm notes of gratitude, and traded family stories with me.

Treat parents with honesty and respect. Relate what their role is, as far as your course is. This is to check that the work is done consistently, to be aware of the grades on tests and on written work, to support the students' efforts to improve and the teacher.

"But, Ma, she wants us to write an essay, and the first draft is due on Monday."

"Then that is what you will do."

Confide your concerns to a parent. "Alan seems very tired in class lately."

"Well, yes, he's working all kinds of hours after school."

"Perhaps he could work a bit less; I'd hate to see his grades drop because he's too fatigued to study."

Or, "Jen's writing certainly has improved."

A parent should NOT, NOT, NOT do the student's work. How does a child learn, or anyone for that matter? Paying attention, attending class regularly, being an active participant—then practice, repetition, study, discussion—and more practice. We all "learn by doing." That sounds so simple.

I will never fathom why a parent does not understand that writing the paper for the student teaches the student

-TANN

nothing. Nothing. Creating the project for the student may get a better grade for the offspring, but the child has learned zilch. If a student is struggling, yes, a parent can help—a bit. Then the parent should tell his son or daughter that he or she should tell the teacher that he didn't understand, he couldn't get it, couldn't do it well and needs help—please.

With practice, a student learns—and can take pride in his work, his improvement. As a parent, do you really want your child to take pride in the fact that you did the work for him? Repeating myself here? It bears repeating.

41. BE ORGANIZED IN THE PLANNING

To integrate and coordinate all the pieces, like those of a fantastic puzzle, takes organization: time and planning. Starting with a then recent article (mentioned previously) in the *Boston Globe* on the vulgarity of teenagers' favorite lyrics, I used a variety of materials. I found lyrics from my generation's songs, comparing the words and the messages to three, currently popular tapes. I first constructed a lesson on the journalist's column, the vocabulary within the column, the use of a lead, and the literary devices he utilized, which were many and quite artful. It was a powerful column by Mike Barnicle, exposing, as it were, the language that millions of teens listened to.

We discussed, quite heatedly at times, not only the different mores, at least as expressed in the songs, of the generations, but also the reasons they had for buying such songs. What could be the rationale for nice, young people, which they were, listening to and purchasing tapes, which contained such vulgarity, invective, violence, and abuse of women and others? To me, it was incomprehensible.

It was an illuminating lesson for me. I had forgotten how young, how childlike many of them were. They loved the songs that spoke of beating up one's girlfriend, of calling her every low-down, disgusting, dirty word one could imagine.

They thought the songs that sung of beating up one's mother, of kicking and stomping on her, were "fun." Why?

They praised the originality of the emotions, the pounding rhythms, and "the honesty." Shocking me was also a small "kick" for them. What further amazed me was that they all played these "ditties" in their homes; their parents knew this, for the most part, and many regarded it as meaningless, youthful exuberance.

Overreacting is what the *Globe* journalist and I engaged in, according to them. They were entranced with the beat, the flouting of authority, and the originality. They contended that the words did not express their feelings or actions at all, but that they could "understand some of "the Black experience" through these songs.

We talked and wrote a great deal about positive values, about virtue, and about respect. I used a myriad of "tools": columns, interviews, discussions, tapes, and their journals, which led to their own creative writing. It took careful monitoring and planning, time, and organization.

42. USE A VARIETY OF MATERIALS AND METHODS TO HELP THEM LEARN AS INDIVIDUALS.

There are a plethora of methods and materials: books, stories, poems, plays, magazines, newspapers, board work, displays, paintings, audio tapes, CD's, movies, videos, old records, and websites. Invite community members, business leaders and homemakers, as well as colleagues, to share their experiences and expertise with the class. Take your classes to movies and museums. Utilize oral presentation, memorization, silent and oral reading, group work, their illustrations, seminar work, portfolios, quizzes, tests, journals, homework, class discussion, their own creative writing. So many sources, so many references, and so many choices to keep you and them excited about learning.

A myriad of ways abounds for you to vary the lessons,

to pique their interests, to cajole the reluctant learner, and to light up the classroom. And, no, the flush of euphoria doesn't occur every day. Time is needed for drill, for "learning to walk before they can fly."

A teacher should contemplate how can I get this lesson across, of what can I avail myself to help them nail this down, to make this bit of instruction theirs?

43. THEIR JOB IS TO TRY: TO BRING A LEVEL OF INTEREST TO THE LEARNING EXPERIENCE, TO LISTEN, TO PARTICIPATE, TO STUDY—TO DO THE WORK. TELL THEM THAT.

You are in charge. They should "learn the ropes" of society. I used to tell them that no one knows what's in your heart, what you are thinking; but your outward appearance says a great deal. This means that those young faces before you have the obligation to learn how to present themselves, to focus on whoever is speaking, to avoid the look of ennui, to look attentive.

A teacher told me that in his class several students sat with bored expressions, never paid attention to the lesson, and simply looked elsewhere when he was speaking. They slouched in their chairs, fiddled with whatever was on the desk, and seemed to want him to know that they were not listening to him. **It's the I-dare you-to teach-me mode.** He was intimidated and also felt he had "no right to tell them to change this 'quiet behavior.'" Wrong.

It is your duty, your obligation not to allow such demeanor in your classroom. Say it loudly and clearly, allowing no disagreement—for there can be none. Students must "look alive"; this means that they owe to themselves, their parents, their teachers, and peers, decent and polite behavior and the appearance, at least, if not the actuality, of trying to learn. Do not quibble or allow an argument about this, nor permit the administration to dissuade you on this. **If disre-**

spectful behavior is allowed or ignored, it spreads like kudzu. And, think about it; if you condone this improper behavior and/or attitude, you help that child rob himself of learning. It's one thing for him to do it; it's another for you look away.

This again is one of those reminders you offer your pupils. You are there to help them improve their knowledge, their skills in your subject. They are there to try, which means to be alert, to participate in the discussion, to do the homework, and to study. There's that microcosm-of-life theory. You each have your jobs. **You are the teacher.**

44. TEACHERS ARE REGULARLY GIVEN OTHER SUPERVISORY DUTIES (IN THE CORRIDOR, THE BATHROOMS, THE BUS, STUDY HALL, OR THE CAFETERIA). DON'T JUST STAND THERE. WALK AROUND, TALK TO THE STUDENTS, ENFORCE THE RULES, AND ANSWER THEIR QUESTIONS. BE ALERT.

Seeing your students in other settings is helpful and often illuminating. If you attend an athletic event or extra curricular activity, you learn about your charges' other skills. Mary turns out to be an accomplished vocalist with the belt-'em-out style of Ethel Merman. Who knew? Kevin is an accomplished wrestler and a team leader. Strolling, while on lunch duty, you see some students not eating at all. Upon investigation, you learn there's a whole table of girls "just dying to be thin." They, unbeknownst to their families, never eat lunch. You talk to them about this, and you report it to the nurse and the administrators.

In the school community, whether it be in your classroom or the lunchroom, or the corridor, for that matter, you may become aware of the loner. A child who is hurting in some way—never speaks to anyone, stays by himself, or seems angry much of the time—should receive your attention.

103

Speaking to the student to try to find out what's going on would be followed up with a visit to the guidance counselor. You or she would call the parents. There are steps that must be taken, rather than ignore this behavior.

A teacher suggested that, perhaps, the reticent child is merely shy. Perhaps. It is better, however, to get involved and find out whether the student feels isolated or has a problem. A loner or a hostile student requires some intervention. A student who is teased or taunted or ridiculed needs help from you, the counselor, and/or the specialists. Bad behavior, I repeat, does not disappear. You have to take steps to stop it and there are many experienced people in your building to help you help that child.

The shy student may need someone to talk to or may benefit from an introduction to the teacher sponsor of an extra-curricular club to get him interested in an activity and to meet other students.

Your presence in the bathrooms or in the corridor may help avoid situations of harassment or fighting. Talk to the students; you get to know many more youngsters, and they get to know you. Be involved.

45. DON'T MERELY BRUSH ASIDE YOUR OWN MIS-CONCEIVED AND/OR ENTRENCHED NOTIONS. DON'T BE CAVALIER ABOUT YOUR PREJUDICES. DEAL WITH THEM.

Some teachers, very few, cross the line of intelligence, of fair play, or of good taste in their remarks. These young minds, sitting before them, absorb casual comments and discussions. In other words, they get the message. Teachers who cross the line should be reported, warned, and then, if these comments continue, dismissed.

- "I know that this may be chauvinistic of me, but I feel that the girls in class enticed those boys to make those lewd remarks and to engage in the touching because of their attire. Those short skirts they wear . . . they know what will happen."

- "We all know that girls get away with so much due to their flirting."
- "Men need to feel that they're in charge, but these career women today are just ruining it."
- "It's a known fact that boys are smarter than girls; you just have to deal with it."
- "Sit that big, round bottom in a chair, you beautiful thing."
- "I understand why gay people offend you."

And these—from teachers!

46. TAKE ON ONE (PAID) EXTRA CURRICULAR ACTIVITY

Being an advisor of an activity, a class, or a group is rewarding, in that you get to know the youngsters in a less formal, less structured setting; and they, in turn, get to know you. It is very time-consuming to help the Student Council, or the 9th grade class, or to sponsor the school newspaper, etc.; but it is great fun. It is so fulfilling to see another side of them—and of you.

You perform a valuable service, giving them a fresh outlet for their energy and creativity; you earn extra money, as well. Also, you gain new skills; you meet more students; and you have an opportunity to view your students in new ways.

47. CONTINUE TO BE A LEARNER YOURSELF: READ NEWSPAPERS, BOOKS, MAGAZINES; GO TO MOVIES, CONCERTS, AND PLAYS; WATCH TV; KEEP UP WITH THE RESEARCH.

Your learning should be ongoing; it doesn't end with your getting the job, or, for that matter, getting comfortable in it. The same advice I would give a computer expert or the purveyor of insurance or a stay-at-home mom—for that matter, anyone—get interested in other things, I would also give to a teacher. Round out your education, as well as develop increased expertise in it.

Find out what your students are interested in. You, of course, do not have to share those interests; but be aware. Know how the Celtics are doing, how Pedro is pitching, and what the hot ticket is on Broadway. Ask what movie is their favorite, what book they can relate to, what fictional character they would like to emulate and why. Exchange opinions of your favorite TV shows with them. All of this may help you to communicate with them.

So many teachers look down their noses, as they say with great disdain, "I never watch TV." Well, isn't that just so grand, so scholarly of you? Get down off that high horse and watch "Law and Order," "The Sopranos," and "Frontline," for example. Young people could use your recommendations, and many will appreciate the creativity involved in these fine shows. I forced myself one year to watch "The Ricki Lake Show" because so many of the girls ran home every day to watch it. I was revolted by its appeal to the basest of our instincts, in the exploitation of those who knew no better or would do anything for a buck. We could then discuss the show, however, (and I could try to figure out what these lovely, young ladies saw in this piece of pander) because I promised them I would watch.

It's also helpful that you energize yourself with new things, sweet pleasures, because the work is often rife with stress. Exercise, make a fun recipe, take a walk.

48. LISTEN TO THE SUCCESSFUL TEACHERS. OBSERVE IN THEIR CLASSES

Some teachers accomplish helping to create students, real students, those who realize that to get a high grade takes effort, takes study. They also maintain a classroom of respect and vivacity. Sit in on their classes, and you will hear them crack a joke, yes, and a smile; but, more importantly, these teachers want their charges to become scholars, mini experts, if you will, which is why their students clearly understand that the work, the homework, the proper demeanor—all are important. Watch these teachers at work; pick up the signals; soak in the atmosphere; spend some time listening, exchanging ideas, and asking questions.

Remember that the pay isn't high, but it's far too high for a babysitter or an amateur entertainer. **You are a professional; you are a teacher.** Pick up pointers from the best.

49. THIS IS A DEMANDING JOB. GET REST AND RELAXATION—AND PLEASURE FROM YOUR LIFE

Edna St. Millay said, "Love is not all." Your job, whether it is a teacher, a software guru, a businessperson, a doctor—should not be all there is of your life. Teaching "is not all." I again advise: take a walk, exercise, paint, or cook a great meal. Invite friends to join you for dinner, play golf, watch TV, rent a movie, go to a museum, indulge your hobby, shop, nap—whatever gives you a change of pace, a breather, a good feeling—do it.

50. ENJOY YOUR STUDENTS. ENJOY YOURSELF

Your students, the greater number of them, will fill you with an exhilaration that makes you feel so alive. You will value what you do and be proud of your work—what more can one ask? I have been so amused by their comments, their stories. I have been so moved by their outpouring of emotion. I have been so impressed at what can, in point of fact, happen, how well and how much they can actually learn when they realize that you "mean business" and/ or when you help to light that spark within them.

It is rather a quid pro quo arrangement, if you think

———

107

about it. It's as if you said to your students, "You give the work and me a chance, your attention and your study; and I will present the material in a varied and interesting way. I will be fair, intelligent, creative, trustworthy, organized, and demanding. I will expect you consistently to behave and to try to do your best. You may feel free to be the real you—that smart, inventive, expressive, honest person, who will be judged as an individual."

Imagine the outpouring of creativity that is emitted by the teacher and the student; imagine how pleasurable, how inspirational this is to all of you, working together. Revel in it. I did.

51. SMILE, GRIN, LAUGH, SHARE—WHAT AN IMPORTANT JOB YOU HAVE. DO IT WELL AND ENJOY THE JOURNEY.

You are a person, who is entitled to love your job; to be an advocate for your students' scholarship; to seek excellence within yourself, your students, your school, and your profession. In the maelstrom that surrounds the testing of students and the testing of future teachers and working teachers, it is possible to get caught up in the frenzy. In the well-intentioned, but sometimes misguided, efforts to make computers and/or testing the prime focus of learning, perhaps some may lose their way. Not you. **You will try to "keep your eyes on the prize": the challenge and the joy of teaching.**

* * *

YOU NEVER ASKED,
BUT . . .

My advice will not waiver very much with time, but the pendulum will, more than likely, swing forward and back, forward and back, on education reform, the type and value of state and national testing, technology in the classroom, etc. Allow me to offer my reactions to some current issues facing education.

Public education has to cross class lines, cultural lines, and economic lines. How much money one has should not determine how good an education his children receive. I believe the same should be true of health care.

We must construct a public school system that does such an admirable job that is so fine, that, not only do foreign countries admire it, we do. People in our cities and towns, in suburbs and rural areas, the rich and the not-so rich, the middle classes, and the poor—everyone is proud of its excellence.

Think of what a gift public education has been to so many. Thousands of people, who today own their businesses and their second homes, succeeded, in large measure, due to public schools. These sons and daughters, grandsons and granddaughters, of immigrants, of laborers and peddlers and drummers, have "made it"—and came then to believe that their children, their grandchildren can receive a good education only in private school. So many have told me that their children are "so smart," so gifted, that they had to send them to "country day." They have become, if not the nouveau riche, the yuppie rich. They turned their backs, in many cases, on neighborhood schools, years before there was the need to do so.

It used to irritate me that they became oblivious to what a fine job the public schools did. And they did.

Now, I am sad to say that, though in the past they were wrong in their lack of confidence in public schools, today their assessment is more accurate.

Is that true of all schools? By no means. There are public schools that shine, some in the suburbs, some in the city. The point is that there are simply too few that do that superlative job that our children need. In an episode of "West Wing," a White House aide is tossing around an expression that he is aware is hyperbole. He is trying to convince a character on the show that he is committed to public education, so he grins and effuses, "Our schools should be palaces." And so they should.

Take a poll of all the legislators, federal and state, and find out who sent their own children to public schools. If they were not good enough for Mr. Secretary, Mrs. Representative, Ms. Senator—Mr. President—they are not good enough for all our children, as well.

MCAS—'TIS "THE CART BEFORE THE HORSE"

MCAS—Massachusetts State testing is, indeed, welcome and needed; national testing, however, should be developed to supplant it someday. There should be a core of knowledge, of skills that are representative of what the country contends its young people should learn. Students in Massachusetts and those from North Carolina, for example, should have common curricula, which would, of course, leave time and place for the individual states or schools or towns, and, yes, teachers to have their local issues and "specialties" included.

MCAS are too long, receive too much emphasis, are too costly, and take up too much time with too many hours of classroom learning missed. Fifteen hours? Seventeen hours? Then, after all this time devoted to testing and test preparation, practice sessions, practice questions and practice tests, only English and math scores are "counted?"

MCAS: "The cart before the horse." The test logically should ascertain if the students are learning what the state has determined they should. Therefore, it stands to reason, schools should not be spending inordinate amounts of time "preparing" students to take the test. Yet, there are test prep programs in place before school, after school, during the summer, in each discipline, and in each class. Why? The presi-

---

111

dent of Bard College dubbed it well, "the tyranny of testing."

Clifford Hill, a professor at Columbia Teachers College, wrote in the *New York Times*, about "the invasion of test prep materials," stating, "Learning to take reading and writing tests is not the same as learning to read and write."

The test should be what it was designed to be, an evaluator of student competency in what we deem important for them to learn. It should answer the question, "Are students demonstrating proficiency in those courses designated in the curricula and on the test as mandatory: English, math, history, science, and foreign language?"

Are the curricula for each school, as manifested in the frameworks (which were approved by the State Department of Education), working? Are the students learning? Are the frameworks encompassing the skills the students need? Is each school, each teacher doing the job well?

Then, using the results, perhaps, we could figure out how to help the low-achieving schools, how to improve teaching methods, and how to assist those students who are not learning well or learning enough. Those are the reasons for which the test was introduced.

Instead, we have a frenetic atmosphere that borders on chaotic, where administrators and teachers put help sessions in place, as well as teacher seminars and courses, all calculated to help students pass the test. They should know that the test is secondary—it's the proverbial cart.

The learning that is going on, day after day, the learning is the horse. Aren't we supposed to derive from this testing experience how well the schools are doing? Aren't the test results tools we can utilize to improve our courses, our methods, our teacher training, our materials, our funding? Any or all of these could benefit from a careful—and fair—analysis of the test scores. What we do is diminish the concept for which the test was initiated by all this extra "padding."

The passing score, with all the qualifying rationales, is one point above failing; and the failure point is kept so low a student is seriously impaired not to pass. Whoop-dee-doo! At present, only the English and the math scores are considered in the pass/fail concept. How sad. Yes, the directors of the state testing, along with many administrators, don't want to appear unfair, so they tell us. They, therefore, have removed other subjects from consideration, along with the lowering of the bar, stating that the test is new.

And what if they had held to the consideration of all the tested subjects and the original idea of what constituted passing? Then teachers, parents, and students alike might grow to respect a process that would extol scholarship, standards, and study. Now we have much ado—attention, emphasis, courses, practices, hours, and dollars—invested in a test that does not deserve special regard.

WHEN WAS THE LAST TIME YOU READ OR HEARD THE WORD "STUDY"? In all the brouhaha of the testing, studying as a routine practice among our students was—and is—rarely, if ever, discussed. We must get across to today's youngsters that drill, that repetition that allows things to become easier, if not second nature, is a learning tool. How else does one become proficient (a category in the MCAS scores) without practice, without drill, without study?

Computers are wondrous machines; I love what I have learned to do via their technology—and I'm continually learning, a novice still. To be moved, impacted, familiarized, etc., by words, by ideas, that is learning. To spend time analyzing a problem; doing research; evaluating an event, a law, a person's influence—that is studying, with a computer or not. It's the process of thinking that is important.

We hear of practice questions and practice exercises and practice essays. Teach; impose a classroom atmosphere that encourages respect for ideas, for study, for discussion, and the exchange of information. Give to them the tools for comprehension: the material, the homework, the writing assignments, the word attack skills, the drill and discussion, buttressed by the computer, the library, and study skills. Stop pretending this rush to have the scores look good to the community is tantamount to improving education.

We must use the test to identify and help those students who do not do well, but we must begin this process when they are very young. Having talented, experienced teachers in the classroom, having smaller classes in those courses or schools where this would be a benefit, having enough guidance counselors, enough quality books and materials, well-maintained buildings constitutes a basic checklist. The chances are that if these factors are "not up to snuff," the students will not do well on the state tests.

The test results must be returned to the students, the parents, and the teachers with far more precision and rapidity than is accomplished currently. Here is a place where the computer could be so very beneficial and efficient. If students take the tests in May, and the results are not known until November or December, this is a major hindrance. Tests someday administered by computer could be "graded" immediately. Returning the results earlier would enable the school and the teacher to focus on what whole classes didn't learn or retain, what individual students need assistance in. The curriculum could be reexamined, and the students could concentrate on improving the skills. These results must be utilized to help.

We have to say it often to our students: that we want them to learn and enjoy learning, that we want them to use what they learn to help them succeed and be happy in their lives. The tests, we must remind them, are barometers that help us help them. And then we have to show them that we're not "full of my hooey," as my father would say.

When they see books tattered and torn, or they don't have enough books; when they see walls that are peeling,

desks that are gouged, don't you think they know the truth? When they have "bad teachers" or no homework, don't you think they realize what's going on? When they can get by with little-to no-preparation, they understand all too well. When there are no library materials, or few computers, no field trips or assemblies, they know words are not deeds and that, maybe, they are not as important as the politicians keep saying they are.

TEACHER TESTING

The large number of prospective teachers failing the teacher tests delivered a wake-up call to those hoping to become teachers, to schools, and universities. Inadequate preparation at all levels was the main culprit. How many times do you believe a person should be allowed to take the test? It is a mockery of a much-needed condition to teach to allow students to take the test again and again and again. Twice. That's it, twice. If you don't pass the test in two tries, choose another career; everyone wasn't cut out to teach.

Former Governor Cellucci of Massachusetts initially proposed testing all current teachers, as well. Not a bad idea to test teachers every five or ten years, perhaps. He seemed to have softened on that idea, and the state is now proposing testing the math teachers of those classes that fail the math MCAS test. How about testing all the teachers in all the failing schools?

This, I know, sounds so reasonable to the public. It ignores, however, some facts. Teachers in more affluent communities have less problems teaching those who are better nourished, better nurtured, better prepared, etc. The reality, however, is that many of the public schools deal daily with special needs students (those with physical, emotional, and/ or mental handicaps), those with behavioral problems, the "children of many languages," the children of the poor and uneducated; and they deal with them in abundance.

Many systems struggle with inadequate funding and simply do not have enough—enough counselors, enough teachers. Some districts use rhetoric to justify complete inclusion (whereby many special needs students are "included" in classes that they clearly cannot handle academically). The special needs student gets little-to-nothing from the class in far too many instances. And the teacher and the class act as babysitter for these students, who are in need of a specialists, small classes, and work from which they can learn. It costs.

Teachers have high expectations for all their students. We have to come to their aid with increased funding and smaller classes in those areas that deserve extra consideration.

Also, we cannot ignore the fact that learning is developmental, that a teacher has students at various levels of proficiency in a class. To hold just that teacher accountable is an error. Let's get back to test them all.

What about the school evaluation process, which in many schools is negligible, at best? Let's hold administrators accountable; let's take a school survey in each building each year, so principals and assistant principals can get feedback from the teachers as to their own effectiveness. Let us have the school committees and the superintendents aware of who has evaluated the teachers, how many times, what were the results, and what were the follow-up procedures. Ineffective teaching skills, poor discipline, and inadequate administration within every building and every class must be addressed.

TECHNOLOGY

The computer is a magnificent instrument (not an over statement) for students to use, organizing their papers, locating a multiplicity of sources, comparing and contrasting both ideas and opinions, communicating with others, and more. **For all its wonders, and they are myriad, the computer is a tool.**

Again, when was the last time you read or heard the word "study" in relation to the goals of the MCAS or in relation to the computer? We must remember to emphasize study and reflection. That is worth repeating. The concept of studying, of reflecting on the information gathered must not only be promulgated to students, but made mandatory. There really isn't a way to speed up the thought process. You can use all the high-tech equipment imaginable to distribute your thoughts. It's thinking itself that eats up all the hours," writes Ellen Goodman in the *Boston Globe*. Although she is referring to journalists in the world of the "new media," the same is true of students

The computer doesn't learn for you. It will help you gather and organize the items to learn; but, in order for the facts, the ideas, and the opinions to be yours, the student still must do the studying, the thinking.

The turn of phrase, the writing style, that voice of yours— they should all be yours. They are developed through trial and error, through much experimentation, many tries.

"Garbage in, garbage out." Teachers are confronted with

---

a large number of pages that students put together from various sources on the Internet and computer programs, as well. There is such a vast array of information out there, and now it is so accessible that students pass in voluminous reports, mistaking quantity for quality. Instead of their own voices, they glom on to the many experts.

Students are constantly told of the wonders of the Net; they can see for themselves politicos literally falling all over themselves, promising to "wire every school and every classroom." Politicians, school committee members, administrators, and CEO's, among others, shout, "Technology is King," and shout it loudly and often. One morning on TV, former Vice President Gore was trumpeting that all homes in America should have access to the Internet. He looked out at the crowd somberly and said, "It can be done." Each day there are a dazzling number of plans set forth by officials and educators and business people, as well, to give to all school children a computer of their own.

This is admirable. I, too, have become a computer devotee, a Dell/MSN junkie. But when will all these people herald studying, hard work, and exemplary behavior? The word is not "computers"; it is what computers can aid you to do at times—learn. **"Learn" is the word. "Study" is the word.**

In the moving tribute, "My Favorite Teacher," (1/9/01) *New York Times* columnist Thomas L. Friedman wrote, "The Internet can make you smarter, but it can't make you smart. It can extend your reach, but it will never tell you what to say at a PTA meeting. These fundamentals cannot be downloaded. You can only upload them, the old-fashioned way, one by one, in places like Room 313 at St. Louis Park High."

Truth be told, technology is a precious asset to the King; but the King is, in fact, learning. Could we possibly be more vocal about studying, about learning? **Could we, indeed, praise the computer and also laud the virtues of homework, of study, of doing one's own original work?** Just copying information gathered from the computer and putting one's name at the top is not a paper. We should not train our young and clever students to be young and clever plagiarists.

Let as applaud computers and all their software applications and accessories for the remarkable achievements they are, arguably right up there in achievement with the Guttenburg press. **LET US BE COGNIZANT THAT IT IS THE MIND THAT IS THE MOST WONDROUS OF INSTRUMENTS.**

EDUCATION IN THE FUTURE

The Immediate Future (splendid oxymoron, if I ever heard one)

To meet the need for new teachers, to offset the low teacher test scores of so many young prospects, to put excellent teachers in the classroom, let's offer retired teachers part-time jobs. They could teach one or two courses a day or, perhaps, teach twice a week. Ms. History, who retired about a year ago, could teach a World History class, for example, and bring her vast knowledge and experience. She could be treated as what she is, a scholar. An additional incentive to the system is that she, being retired, would receive no additional benefits. Ms. Special Needs could assist with testing or remedial programs, helping part-time with the existing burgeoning workload.

Retired teachers may know the routine of the school and some of the teachers and students. Of course, administrators would choose only those who were fine, enthusiastic teachers before they retired, those who knew well their subject and created an atmosphere of learning. They should be paid more than you would a cleaning professional or a burger flipper and given the respect they earned. Regard them as consultants, as experts—because they are.

It always piqued that outside experts and consultants, many of whom were less engaging or knowledgeable than some of the faculty members with similar expertise, were treated with great obeisance, as well as hefty remuneration. The familiarity of the administrators with the staff members seemed to be an impediment to seeing their proficiency and, thereby, utilizing them as "in-house" consultants.

Retired teachers could act as mentors to new teachers, which would help during that first year, when so much is required of them. I enjoyed my mentoring and my teaching and could have been enlisted to do one or both on a part-time basis.

THE ARTS—MONEY AND MOUTH

We preach, actually expound, about the concept of art appreciation, but do not make it, when it easily could be, a reality. Let's put a small amount of our money where our mouth is. Art is important? Beauty is important? Nature is important? Let us "show, rather than tell."

Paintings should be prominently displayed everywhere, in classrooms, in corridors and on bulletin boards, and in the offices. Sculpture, photos, drawings, and paintings should exist in a school environment. Of course, they'll be reproductions; but they'll be seen, recognized, appreciated. Flowers and plants should be placed around the building, as well. No, no, no, not the teachers schlepping them in from home to their own classrooms and not just in the science teachers' classrooms.

When I suggested this so many years ago, I was told of budget constraints. Posters and plants cost very little and should be included in the budget; they are considered extras or frills because of a mind-set and because we have allowed it. How do you help give the students a bit of that soft texture of life, the beauty that helps us see and feel?

I don't want to hear snickers or poo-pooing. We clamor about "the arts," yet we manifest that our words are just that—words. Let them smell lilacs (perhaps not as catchy as "Let them eat cake.") and surround them with loveliness.

———

122

The world is often seen as harsh; let us create for them, while we can, an ambience of color, aroma, and beauty. They should be able to recognize famous representative work. Because they're young or poor, or not scholastically bent—because we can't afford it, etc., can no longer be used as excuses. Can we afford not to? And, think about it, in all these years we have not done it. Speaking about "the same old, same old" being entrenched . . . Let's shake it up—and, keep in mind, these are very small steps.

In a similar vein, groups of musicians and actors and artists should present their talents to the student body on occasion. Performances by professionals, college students, other towns' groups, as an exchange program—all should be encouraged to make students aware of talent and skill, just the sheer pleasure of the artistry. Many young people have rarely, if ever, attended performances; and some, consequently, also need to learn the appropriate behavior. Experience and exposure are important. Think of a jazz quintet entertaining or an operatic aria being performed then discussed and explained by way of the technique or the training required.

SPEAKERS—CAREERS

And let's hear from those CEO's, who so frequently complain to the press about the schools. Owners of businesses in the area could come into the classrooms during or after school to acquaint students with their own jobs, their companies, the training and education that they would recommend. They could sign up some of their employees to act as mentors, as they could themselves. New apprentice training programs could be generated, whereby each owner would agree to take on, at least, one student as a trainee or part-time employee. We read of so many CEO's making large salaries and their companies being ever more profitable. Let each business leader also "put his money where his mouth is." Criticism may, in many cases, be deserved; but lead, help; "don't just stand there."

THE NO-SO DISTANT FUTURE—HORACE MANN MEETS ISAAC ASIMOV

To believe that education will remain much as it is now is short sighted and naïve. It has needed a push, actually a kick, for years now. The school in which I taught differed from the school I attended (a million years ago) probably in only four ways. It offered a couple more courses. It was, and is, rife with an atmosphere of rah-rah, the students-should-enjoy-themselves, let's-have-fun. It categorized as "honor" students and "college" students, those who clearly were not, due to a small enrollment, lack of funds, and the desire to promulgate a positive public image. And it was disingenuous about scholarship, creating a climate that did not encourage excellence, in academics nor behavior, while contending that scholarship was the primary reason for its existence.

The fundamental classroom arrangements were the same, the courses, the departments, the room configurations, the order of class periods, etc. The addition of the computer and computer classes are, of course, welcome additions to today's schools.

Schools need some fresh air, some experimentation, which I believe will come, with or without educators initiating them. One concept that I had discussed with my students was the question of the need for high schools at all—in the distant future.

With the dismal record of many schools, the fact that a large number of upper-class students have part-time jobs, the improving technology, and the lack of teaching excellence, there should be a hew and cry for new approaches.

The "virtual school" (if not high school juniors and seniors, then, most assuredly, college students) might be a novel idea worthy of consideration "down the road a piece." I vividly remember discussing Isaac Asimov's story "The Fun They Had" with my classes. It was in connection with our projects on the future, and it was one of the works in a science fiction unit. Perhaps, it was an example of education, or irony, or utilized to show again that writers can make statements through, not only non-fiction, but fiction, as well. Here we had education—individual and by computer—in a world where books had simply disappeared. Books had gone the way of the quill pen or writing on birchbark, or, in my elementary-school days, inkwells.

The prolific Asimov has the children of the future wistfully long for neighborhood schools, group education, heterogeneous grouping, and being taught by a "real teacher," not a machine. Little Margie and her friend Tommy are awe-struck, upon finding a book, that the print remains on the page and that "in the olden days" everyone learned together. "Now" they learned with "a machine" in their separate homes, potentially seven days a week, rain or shine, I imagine. The author makes his statements with warmth about the advantages of public schools, as his fictional future children read the diary of the children of the "past" and think of "the fun [we must have] had." What a prophet he was.

Today, almost fifty years after the story was written, our vision has altered. To give him his due, Mr. Asimov appreciated and "predicted" the sophistication, widespread use, and ease of computer learning. He, no doubt, might have taken it to his own bosom. Now, we exalt computer education; individual learning; "books on machines"; and working on our computers at home, at work, and at school, not to mention in cafes, airplanes, and airports.

It is a "brave new world." Michael Saylor, described in the *Washington Post* as a "high-tech billionaire," made headlines with his vision to donate $100 million to create a high-caliber virtual university, available to everyone in the world without charge. What a thrilling concept. How generous, how viable. Why not a virtual high school?

Before you hug what we have now because it is familiar, let's remember the need for that fresh air. Recall, if you will, the thundering criticism of our public schools, which, in large measure, precipitated the development of curriculum frameworks, of MCAS, of statewide assessments. Keep in mind the glaring need to close the gap between the rich and the poor.

How about community centers, (yes, in the far-off future, perhaps) shared by two or three towns, that offer to high school juniors and seniors a supervised place to get counseling, to socialize, to participate in sports, to study, to use computers, to get study assistance, driver training, and job training?

Courses would be designated by the state and the regional communities and taught via the computer. The main course work would be done, a la Isaac Asimov, at home. Testing could be by the computer or at the community centers.

At "my" virtual high school and Mr. Salor's virtual university, the computer-generated courses would be taught by the best, the most talented, the most interesting, learned teachers from all over the world. Think of the excitement.

We could "erase" those town lines, and, perhaps, eventually, save money—less teachers, less schools, etc. Centers could be open from 7 in the morning or not open 'til noon, as districts establish their needs and goals. Maybe the agenda would be for the students to do their computer work at home, the centers not opening until 12 or 1 in the afternoon. They could remain open 'til 10 or 11 in the evening and have food courts for dining or snacking (or to train future chefs in food preparation).

Dances and performances could take place at the center. The fine arts, which always get short shrift in most schools, art and music and drama and dance, could be offered and encouraged for every "member." A gymnasium with machines, coaches, and daily exercise would be part of the routine schedule. Regular field trips could be initiated by the center to museums, to other towns, to performances, to other community centers.

Each young person would have a mentor/counselor to help construct a well-rounded program of selections. Mandatory would be an atmosphere of respect, of cordiality, of scholarship. There would be "quiet rooms" for study, a media center, gymnasium, craft rooms, fine arts rooms, and a computer lab. Futuristic? Certainly.

Education is a slow learner itself, and my suggestions for those upper level high schoolers was precipitated, in part, by the fact that schools now realize that the MCAS testing (state testing) will be mostly completed by the 10th grade. Therefore, there will be, I predict, a hodgepodge of electives and career training programs, a sort of marking time for juniors and seniors until they are graduated, initiated by the schools. Instead, let's get ready for the "new education."

HERE COMES OUR "BRAVE NEW WORLD"—GET READY

The virtual college education, the soon-to-be explosion of courses and training programs for some who, heretofore, entered college will, I have no doubt, herald in a revolution in education—as it should. There will be adults of every age at ease by their computers, availing themselves of degrees, or illumination, job training, and skill acquisition. It will be extraordinary.

Imagine how astoundingly successful these college offerings—virtual school or no, would be if, in fact, the students of all ages were well prepared in their youth by skilled, knowledgeable, and dynamic teachers!

ADDENDUM

VOUCHERS— AND CHARTER SCHOOLS— AND LEARNING

I must confess I never understood the concept of vouchers, nor, for that matter, charter schools. If you had a company that was not doing well, would you fix it? Would you, instead, build a similar company that would require funds and manpower, while leaving the floundering company to continue to fail in its mission?

Vouchers, here in Massachusetts, are seen by some, in part, as a method to give money to parochial schools. After all, the reasoning goes, those who pay taxes and then choose to send their children to parochial schools (for religious reasons, they purport), are, in fact, paying twice. A sizeable number of Catholics choose to have their children educated with children who have like backgrounds. They feel that way their offspring are safer, get better discipline, and better education. Would that it were so.

On the whole, there is, with some exception, no evidence that parochial education is superior. The discipline is better only in the fact that they have the luxury to have offending students expelled (thrown back to the public schools, of course).

133

Vouchers throughout the country, and evidently supported by Democrats and Republicans in like number, are a betrayal of public education. To repeat, and it does bear repeating, I never really understood the concept of vouchers. If a school is a dismal failure, as evidenced by continual, low test scores, by inadequate books, inadequate teaching, inadequate materials, inadequate support, a climate of violence, send in a team to upgrade it—or close it down. To offer parents vouchers, so they can send their children to other—and better—schools seems disingenuous. Fix the "offending" school. Pour expertise and rigor and, yes, funds into that school. Solve the problems; don't merely compound them by removing students and the funds to educate them.

Politicians get votes by hopping on the voucher bandwagon. Parents get excited that they can send their children to a better learning environment. Some take that voucher and "carry" it to a parochial or a private school, having to make up the difference in tuition that both charge. Private and parochial schools covet the funds; for they, too, have to pay their bills.

Think of the Metco Program, which began many years ago in Boston, and which, with state funding, enabled minority students from Boston schools to attend suburban schools. The students, indeed, then attended better schools in safer neighborhoods. The program also afforded the students from the suburbs to have a more diverse student body. It is hoped, surely, that both groups learn from and with one another.

It is many years later, and Metco still thrives. Have the schools these students left improved? The value of a diverse student body is undeniable. Would the Metco students, however, have preferred to remain in their own neighborhood schools had the institutions been "up to snuff?" The schools, in many cases, were run down, had textbooks that were few and many that were obsolete, were populated by students who were allowed to "get by." An atmosphere prevailed that was unsafe and uninspiring, to say the least. Thus, the birth of Metco ensued—and continues today—with city kids fanning out to the greener pastures of the suburbs.

The parents of private and parochial students feel they are being short changed, having to pay tuition, as well as taxes that support the public schools, which their progeny do not attend. They opted for better education. It is because we, the government, the citizenry have not insisted upon and consistently maintained what we give lip service to—excellence. Diversity and religion would not even be discussed, in relation to education, had our schools been the jewels, the showcases, the "palaces" that Aaron Sorkin alluded to in "The West Wing."

Thus, we have charter schools springing up in many states, as well, and an ever-growing shout about vouchers from representatives of both parties. **So many politicians, so many of our most prominent leaders contend that they will make education the top priority. The trouble with our schools is, evidently, so complicated, so huge. How else can one explain why, after so many promises, so much money, so much rhetoric, why we have lost faith in public education?**

Our vision is so scattered, so unfocused that we slap bandages on the issues, bandages, such as charter schools and vouchers, and, apparently, seem not to realize that that is what they are, bandages.

State testing is a step in the right direction, but there has to be a commitment, a follow-through. Standards should be set that test the curricula and that test the teaching of those curricula, *not that test the test*. If math and science and English and writing and history are what we believe every student should have the basic knowledge of before leaving our public schools—so be it. After a couple of years of those standards in place, after the public and the students know that "we mean business," students will realize that we, as a nation, want them to have knowledge in what we believe essential to them. These skills, these subjects are important for them to learn in order to cope, to survive, to thrive, and to be citizens of our country, regardless of their state, their city, their race, religion, nationality, or economic level.

You know the old joke of "Who is buried in Grant's tomb?" To hear the "man on the street" interviews on "The Tonight Show" with Jay Leno with so many respondents answering, "Hugh" or "I don't know, never heard of him," may not be a just mirror of our education. But, I must regrettably admit, it's fairly accurate. It makes us weep that this is so. State testing is supposed to eliminate the graduation of students who do not learn those basic requirements that we, as a society, set in place. You want to fool around? You will not graduate. Period.

We need vision and conviction and money. We need talent and intelligence. If a teacher is not a good teacher, she gets retrained, supervised, and becomes a good teacher, or she "gets gone."

If a student chooses not to study, thus not learning the curriculum, he will not do well in class, therefore not do well on the state testing, and thus not graduate. Simple? No. Necessary? Unequivocally. Some students (evidently, far too many) need to "be made" to study, to do the homework, to be participants in the learning process.

The old saying applies here, "The more I practice, the luckier I get." Learning the facts, the processes, the skills— all are necessary. Learning how to learn, the "practice" from the old saying above, is essential.

My students and I marveled at our ever-changing landscape: computers, DVD's, cell phones, cable, the "toys" that have become so much an integral part of our lives. And who, even ten years ago, ever spoke of places like Somalia or Bosnia? **The world changes and so rapidly that it is *learning how to learn* that our education has to provide.**

Our goals must include giving our young people the opportunities to learn how to learn: how to access and utilize information. Assignments, over time, will allow them to become comfortable with the silence that will provide the atmosphere (here comes that word again) to "study." Portfolios and group projects should not replace methods like drill and homework and practice, practice, practice.

The Vice President and Provost of Tufts University, Sol Gittleman, stated in a letter to the editor in the *Boston Globe* (1/21/01), "We have forgotten that there is a process of lifelong learning that needs to be measured so schools can tell whether we have taught them how to learn—not during four years [referring to college testing] but during the forty years after college." The same is true of school education. We must not become obsessed with state testing and scoring. "Keeping [our] eyes on the prize" is our focus. The prize is learning. Yes, I am repeating myself.

How do we "make" them learn? Here comes my "broken record," my recapitulation: fine teachers, intelligent, enthusiastic, and well trained; communication among teachers and between teachers and parents; good materials, varied and up-to-date; fair, firm and consistent discipline; safe and pleasant surroundings; many opportunities to learn, to improve, to excel—and be evaluated; exposure to sports, the arts, and student activities; avenues to guidance and tutoring; at the secondary level, homework on a regular basis—and, for all students, an omnipresent atmosphere of scholarship. Adequate funding that will enable our students to have "all the above" is vital. Bandages won't do.

*   *   *

PT

ACKNOWLEDGMENTS

Gratitude and Thanks:

To A grand group of women for lunches, laughter, and decades of sharing

My brother Jack for his generosity

Leeney for ever-constant caring

Barbara and Jerry and their family for many years of including me and mine

Jeh for hundreds of dinners and endless support

The Lanes, good neighbors and friends

Stan for years of praise and encouragement

The Xlibris staff for gentle assistance

My daughters, Lonni and Julie Tanner, for looking at the world—and at me—and always reaching out to help

~ ~

Phyllis Tanner was the English Department Head for many years in a high school on the south shore of Massachusetts, outside of Boston. She was the recipient of Horace Mann Grants for creating courses in SAT review and Journalism and introducing and sponsoring a school newspaper and a literary magazine. She is a Reading Specialist and a teacher of reading and writing, specializing in journalism, creative writing, and poetry. Currently, she teaches reading and writing courses at Massasoit Community College. Her two daughters also work in community service, in New York City and Washington, D.C., respectively. Ms. Tanner resides in the suburb of Sharon, Massachusetts.